Foe into Friend

Foe into Friend

*The Makers of the New Germany
from Konrad Adenauer to Helmut Schmidt*

Marion Dönhoff

Translated by Gabriele Annan

St. Martin's Press   *New York*

English translation copyright © George Weidenfeld and Nicolson
Ltd 1982
Originally published in German under the title *Von Gestern nach
Übermorgan*
Copyright © Albrecht Knaus Verlag, Hamburg 1981
All rights reserved. For information, write:
St. Martin's Press, Inc., 175 Fifth Avenue, New York, NY 10010
Printed in Great Britain
First published in the United States of America in 1982

ISBN 0-312-29692-4

Library of Congress Cataloging in Publication Data

Dönhoff, Marion, Gräfin.
    Foe into friend.

    1. Heads of state – Germany (West) – Biography.
2. Germany (West) – Politics and government.   3. Germany
(West) – History.   I. Title.
DD259.63.D66   1982   943.087'092'2   82-10381
ISBN 0-312-29692-4

Contents

I
Who are the Germans?

For three decades the frontier between the free world and Communism has run diagonally across the Potsdamer Platz in Berlin. Until 1945 this was the most popular square in Germany's former capital. Today, a wall five metres high crawls through Berlin, and instead of one Germany there are two: the Federal Republic of Germany whose capital is Bonn, and the German Democratic Republic (GDR) which is governed by the communistic SED party.

The leaders of the SED like to emphasize that because of the immense social and economic differences between the GDR and the Federal Republic the inhabitants of the two countries have lost their sense of belonging together. According to this theory the founding of a state of workers and peasants led to the development of a new type of state – their own 'socialist nation' – on an infinitely higher plane than the 'bourgeois nation' of the Federal Republic. In the GDR this idea began to develop only towards the end of the 1960s. As late as 1966 the expression 'two states, but one nation' was still in frequent use: it was used, for instance, in the GDR's application for membership of the United Nations. But only a year later, at the seventh party congress of the SED in 1967, the distinction between '*Staatsvolk*' (members of a state) and '*Nation*' (nation) was introduced. And another year later, in 1968, article 1 of the constitution of the GDR referred to it as 'a socialist state of German nationality'.

It was only gradually that the unique character of the 'socialist nation state' came to be postulated – a state having no connection whatever with the bourgeois nation. Finally,

1

Walter Ulbricht, the First Secretary of the Party, coined the concept of the 'German socialist national state'. And so, from the early 1970s onwards, the government in East Berlin has campaigned against 'claptrap' about the so-called unity of the German nation.

Of course West Germans too have changed their concept over the years. No more than the SED, did the FDR in the beginning imagine that two states were living under one national roof. For a quarter of a century we recognized only one state as the heir and sole representative of the whole former German Reich. In those early days we regarded the German state in the East as an un-state, as the Soviet Zone. All this did not change until the new *Ostpolitik* began in 1970.

Willy Brandt was elected Federal Chancellor in 1969, the first Social Democrat ever to head the government. In his inauguration speech he said: 'Twenty years after the foundation of the Federal Republic and the GDR we must try to stop the two parts of the German nation from drawing even further apart; to find rules for living side by side, and thereby gradually come to live together.' At that time he declared emphatically that the two states could never be foreign countries to one another: their relationship was special. That was the origin of the theory of two German states within one nation, and that is why to this day the FDR has no ambassador in the GDR: instead, each state maintains a 'permanent representative' in the other.

So do the Germans now have two fatherlands? That question shows how far we have moved from our history. No one nowadays uses the word 'fatherland'. No one can bring himself to pronounce it. Not only because during the Nazi period it was perverted and stained with blood, but also because it belongs to a world which no longer exists today. Generations of Germans have lovingly worshipped their fatherland and faithfully revered it – but who can be expected to feel enthusiasm, let alone love, for a rump of a state which in any case is primarily an alliance of expediency, an artificial structure with no capital?

Loyalty is something quite different. The Federal Republic has deserved it and gets it. For this is the freest state that ever existed on German soil, and the society that has developed there is open, liberal, and modern, free from class warfare and chauvinism. The only thing lacking is a national identity: that we do not have. There are no longer any Germans, only 'citizens of the Federal Republic' and 'citizens of the German Democratic Republic'. Imagine a Frenchman or an American unable to say, 'In France, we . . .' or 'We Americans . . .' It is not so easy to live in such a state of abnormality.

On the other hand, one really has to ask whether the Germans were ever as sure of their identity as were the English or the French. Over the centuries, to be 'German' kept on being something different. The picture changes so fast that each generation might be a different people. Once Germans were famous as composers, poets and thinkers, as scientists and scholars. For a long time Germany was the spiritual laboratory of Europe – where most new ideas originated. Karl Marx, Sigmund Freud, and Albert Einstein, the initiators of great discoveries and insights which still define our world today, received their greatest response in Germany. And even then, what happened? First William II and his generation spread terror through the globe and then Germans in brown shirts and hob-nailed boots trampled over the land – until they too disappeared.

'Germany is a land of miraculous revivals and apocalyptic catastrophes,' writes the French historian Pierre Gaxotte. And indeed looking back over the centuries one has to admit he is right. There was the Thirty Years War which left the country in ruins; unity seemed to be lost for ever. But then, in the subsequent wars against the Turks, Austria (then part of the Empire) rose to the position of a great power. True, Napoleon put an end to that empire in 1806, but this decline was again followed by a revival: a number of highly modern states – Prussia, Saxonia, and Württemberg – made their appearance, and when the North German Federation, which in 1867 had united thirty-six states, came to an end, German unity was born with the new Empire of 1871.

In the new century the chain reaction of decline and fall continued. The First World War, in which a whole generation perished, led to an economic crisis such as had never been seen before: the middle classes were impoverished by inflation which finally reached a level where the dollar stood at 4.2 trillion marks. Insanely heavy reparations produced an army of 6 million unemployed. But again, there was an incredible revival. Under Hitler a people that had only recently been brought to its knees rose to extraordinary achievements. The country became the strongest military power in Europe. Hitler, faithful to the silly motto 'the more the enemy, the greater the honour', frivolously challenged the whole world.

In the west the Germans overran the French Maginot Line which experts had regarded as impregnable; in the east they penetrated to the suburbs of Moscow. And then again there followed a complete collapse. This time, people thought, there would be no rise. The Germans lost a quarter of their empire. The rest was divided and West Germany was inundated with more than ten million destitute refugees seeking shelter in her bombed towns and overcrowded villages; and yet what came to be called the economic miracle gradually emerged and amazed the world. The Federal Republic has now become the foremost economic power in Europe.

Thus, in her history, Germany really does seem to be characterized by an ability to rise like a phoenix after an apocalyptic fall. We need not ask about cause and effect, whether the rise leads to the fall or the fall provokes the rise: the decisive factor is that there is a lack of moderation about both. Germans have never had the necessary sense of measure or talent for compromise.

Gaxotte's thesis, then, looks correct. At any rate, there is more truth in it than in the absurd contention, widely held especially since 1945, that there is a straight line leading from Martin Luther through Frederick the Great and Bismarck on to Hitler. People who believe that have never read a word of Luther; they know nothing about Frederick II, they have not the faintest inkling of Bismarck's policy of European balance; nor have they understood how the National Socialists combined mass movement with totalitarian government. Thomas Mann, always critical of the Germans, invoked Luther and Bismarck in the same breath as Goethe, calling them 'the three great Germans who rise like giant mountains . . . from the flattest plain'.

So one of the German characteristics is a strange leaning towards the absolute. In philosophy we find it in Hegel; it was already evident in Kant, and it is often to be found in German literature. It was typical of the Romantic age and the *Jugend* movement at the turn of the century. Our literature is filled with a longing to live life in the absolute: the corollary is contempt for the life of the ordinary citizen who is satisfied with everyday material values. From Kleist to Hermann Hesse and Ernst Jünger many German writers have inclined towards tragedy and melancholy. They were attracted by a longing for absolute truth, for pure doctrine, for uncompromising devotion and personal sacrifice.

In contrast many of today's writers are characterized by a negative, critical, pessimistic attitude. One often feels that they prefer to see the government – whatever the party in power – humiliated by mistakes or defeats, rather than to welcome its positive achievements. They wallow in crises; prosperity within the country or approval from abroad only give them pangs of conscience; and signs of contentment evinced by ordinary people strike them as extremely disturbing.

Ever since Martin Luther, Germans have been characterized by their worship of 'inner freedom'. In the world of practical affairs, this can lead to a perverted kind of individualism. Adolf Lowe has made this very vivid by comparing the Germans with the British, who always strive to avoid extremes. The British principle, he thinks, is never to push an argument to its limit, because that disturbs the spirit of co-operation. German gatherings, on the other hand, can often resemble battlefields. Lowe sums up: 'The price of political freedom is the voluntary limitation of each individual's demands. You cannot have both.'[1]

Over and over again in the course of their history the Germans were magically drawn to distant heights or mystic abysses of one kind or another – more in east Germany than in the west, because the west was more committed to the Enlightenment. German taste likes ideas to be sublime and deeply felt, but not necessarily concrete or practical. Intuition often means more to them than knowledge, and they tend to have more admiration for feeling than for analysis. Many of them find primordial, mythical instincts more interesting than insights with a bearing on reality.

For centuries then, there was no such thing as a German in any real sense of the word. There were Saxons, Bavarians, Prussians – the tribes that had been united in the Holy Roman Empire. When this Empire fell apart in 1806, the nostalgia for it remained, and people went on searching for a framework for the many states and the minute entities that insisted on regarding themselves as states in their own right: there were over seventeen hundred of them altogether. It was not until 1871 that the splinters were reunited in a new political order – the German Empire created by Bismarck.

Alfred Grosser was born a German but grew up as a Frenchman, and knows both nations equally well. He has made some very informative observations on the German concept of a nation by comparing it with the concept in other countries. He thinks that historical circumstances have given German nationalism a conservative, authoritarian direction. In the United States, on the other hand, the nation grew out of the struggle for independence and human rights, and these origins have never disappeared: the Constitution and the Declaration of Human Rights are indissolubly bound together. In France, he thinks, the Revolution created two ideas of nationhood: the left-wing patriotism of the Jacobins, and the right-wing patriotism of the nationalists. This double heritage has enabled the French to make all their conquests with a clear conscience: they were always able to invoke the name of liberty. Alfred Grosser writes:

> In Germany the national idea belonged *successively* to the Right and the Left, but never to both simultaneously. Until the failure of the 1848 Revolution, nationalism and liberalism were united together, if not actually fused. The aim was to unite the nation which hitherto had consisted of small groups of subjects under major or minor rulers, and to set the legitimate sovereignty of the people against the sovereignty of the princes. The three colours of the German Democracy, black, red and gold, were originally the colours of the Jena students' union, whose founders fought against Napoleon in the Wars of Liberation between 1813-15.
>
> But after the failure of the 1848 Revolution, national unity was created by an authoritarian state. It was the government that undertook to found and defend the nation – a nation based on the people, not on the people as a power, however, but on the people as a tribe, as a collection of subjects obedient to their temporal and spiritual rulers. A different kind of tradition might have led to a different development. But the tradition that became dominant under the Empire made no bones about the division of roles: the government gives the orders, and the citizen must cultivate private virtue in his work and in his family: the only public virtue is loyalty to the legitimate ruler.[2]

It was the tradition of the sovereign state that destroyed the Weimar democracy, or rather prevented it from prospering, because people had got into the habit of thinking that governing was a secret science which only the sovereign state could master and practise with the help of a special caste of initiated officials. The power of the civil service was therefore nearly absolute and political parties were dismissed as cliques pursuing their own interests. The mechanism of democracy seemed an insult to venerable traditions.

In the immediate past, positive values have been perverted. In the darkest phase of our history, under Hitler, idealism was twisted into an uncritical belief in authority; adaptability became opportunism; loyalty became servility; and devotion, uncritically pursued to the point of absurdity, finally turned into crime. The Nazi period had a corroding effect on authority and led to permanent disillusionment with it: consequently people today value a critical attitude more highly than anything else. In the long run, this may have a diminishing effect on creativity, but it may spare the Germans further adventures and mistakes.

There are, I think, three factors that have been paramount in shaping the German character. First, the geographical position of the country in the centre of Europe: no other country has so many neighbours and therefore frontiers, and all the problems that that involves, as Germany. Second, the difference in life-styles: in the eastern part this was determined by the East, and in the western by the West. In Europe civilization moved from East to West, which meant in the case of Germany that areas whose history went back to Roman times were joined with others that had not been colonized until the twelfth and thirteenth centuries. And thirdly, there are the two denominations which have always provided a certain amount of tension: Protestantism in the east and north, and Catholicism in the west and south.

So people's fundamental attitudes, their whole way of life, have been quite different according to where they lived. From the time of the Teutonic knights onwards landowners in the east had farmed their own lands, while tenant farming was the norm in the west. The east German landowner therefore acquired the character of an employer, whereas in the west he let off his land and lived off the rent.

From the very beginning life in the west was determined by towns and cities, and quite soon by industry as well. The east, on the other hand, was agrarian. The people of the east therefore developed a degree of social inertia, and a propensity to cling too long to a traditional order and its values. The lack of balance in the German character may derive from the tension inherent in the contrast between east and west, which was never quite resolved.

In the nineteenth and early twentieth centuries, the differences between east and west were most strongly apparent in the field of religion. Prejudice on both sides was colossal. In the Protestant east, the ordinary, not normally very sophisticated, citizen considered all Catholics liars: for, it was said, the Catholic Church trained all its faithful to be hypocrites and pharisees. The *idées reçues* in the west culminated in the belief that heathenism was still rampant in the east. Even in 1980, on the occasion of Pope John Paul II's visit to the Federal Republic, the theological differences were voiced with unexpected force.

In the fateful year 1806 the Austrian Francis I renounced the title of Holy Roman Emperor because the rulers united in the Federation of the Rhine had declared their intention of leaving the Empire. That marked the end of the Holy Roman Empire. From now on, until the Congress of Vienna in 1815, there were three Germanies: Austria, Prussia, and Napoleon's protégé, the Federation of the Rhine.

It was at the beginning of the nineteenth century that Napoleon's hammer blows smashed the European political system. In the resulting changes the Austrian centre of gravity moved south-eastward, and Prussia became the foremost power on the Rhine, although her possessions there were not yet geographically linked with her eastern territories. But the decision taken at the Congress of Vienna to unite the Protestant Hohenzollern state with the Catholic Rhineland was to be decisive for the history of German unification during the nineteenth century. From now on, Prussia was the most important factor in German history, and had a decisive influence on the German character.

The two greatest periods in Prussian history had been the eighteenth century, the age of enlightenment and tolerance; and the period of reform at the beginning of the nineteenth century. During that first period European intellectuals regarded Frederick the Great as the *ne plus ultra* among enlightened monarchs. Voltaire, the most brilliant intellect in

Europe at the time, wrote to his niece in 1740: 'At last I am in Potsdam. Under the late king it was a parade ground, not a garden. The sound of guards marching was the only music, there were military reviews instead of plays, and lists of soldiers instead of a library. Now it is the palace of Augustus, the seat of the finest minds, of pleasure, glory, splendour and taste.'

Prussia gave shelter to the persecuted Huguenots, and also to the religious refugees from Bohemia and Moravia. Frederick II settled people from Salzburg in East Prussia, and he was the first European ruler to abolish torture. Prussian law was considered the most progressive, and for the first time the country had facilities for improving its education and culture. Frederick the Great appreciated the Jesuits as teachers and offered them refuge when their order was expelled from Catholic Europe and finally dissolved by the Pope in 1773. It was he who built the impressive great church of St Hedwig for the Catholics in Berlin, and he never stopped exhorting the two denominations to practise tolerance towards one another.

At the beginning of the nineteenth century, immediately after the Wars of Liberation, and the collapse of her armies at Jena and Auerstedt in 1806–7, Prussia lost half her territories to Napoleon; the whole country was occupied by the French, and the king forced to flee to the remotest corner of his kingdom at Memel: it is astonishing that in spite of all this the country still had the strength for a major revival in the social and intellectual sphere. Sebastian Haffner writes: 'Romantic Berlin began to displace classical Weimar as an intellectual centre. Political and literary personalities mingled in the salons of Rahel Levin and Dorothea Schlegel. There was nothing static or ossified about this world: it was distinguished, intelligent, and witty, and its ideas were modern, progressive, humane, and favourable to reform.'[3]

The absolutist regime was transformed into a modern constitutional state. The reforms of Stein and Hardenberg liberated the peasants and made the cities self-governing;

Humboldt founded the university of Berlin. 'Democratic principles within a monarchy,' said Hardenberg, 'seems to me to be the right formula for the present time.' But the spirit of liberalism was not to flourish long. After the first two decades of the century, Metternich's influence spread reaction throughout Europe, and the age of the Restoration began. No one cared about reform any longer.

Throughout the eighteenth century Prussia had been extremely warlike, but there had been room for enlightenment and free thought. Prussia was a poor country – no one could have regarded her as a potential great power. She had lived beyond her strength. Frederick the Great was very conscious of this: he mockingly suggested that instead of an eagle she should have an ape in her coat of arms, because she only aped the great powers instead of really being one. As Count Mirabeau once wrote, 'Most countries possess an army. Prussia is an army that possesses a state.'

In the nineteenth century Prussia had no choice but to take on the unification of Germany. Bismarck had linked her irrevocably to the German fate. He completed what Frederick II had begun: the founding of a German state opposed to the Habsburgs. This could only be achieved if one of the smaller states could establish itself as a great second power besides Austria. And this in turn would only be possible if everything was concentrated on this one aim and if every other interest was subordinated to politics and the army.

As a result, the importance of military matters was overrated: after all, the German state owed its existence to militarism. This was not so obvious as long as Bismarck was aiming to establish a balance of power in Europe; but later, without his vision and his hand on the tiller, the militarist outlook led to total mindlessness. In the end no one really knew what goals the Emperor William II had in mind or why he wanted to build up his gleaming new army or engage his fast-growing navy. There was no underlying idea, only economic and military greed. Power for power's sake seemed to be the motto of this inane, pseudo-Prussian Wilhelmism.

In a lecture entitled 'The Difficult Fatherland' Rudolf von Thadden, an authority on Prussian history, has given a very striking picture of the German state of mind at the turn of the present century: 'Industrialists and scientists counted for something under the Empire; but the highest respect was reserved for those who were able to add a title or an honour to their names. To be an officer of the reserve became particularly attractive. Obituaries of learned professors would mention that they had been lieutenants in the reserve before they listed the distinguished academies of science to which they had belonged. . . . On the one hand Germany was making every effort to transform herself into a great power with modern technology and a modern army to match; on the other hand she did nothing to develop the necessary structures of responsibility nor the behaviour that should have gone with her newly won power.'

There are certain parallels between the German mentality under William II and under Hitler. Consider the following quotation: 'There will be no pardon. We shall take no prisoners. One thousand years ago the Huns made a name for themselves that still rings powerfully through the ages in folk tale and legend; thus Germany must establish her name in such a manner that never again shall anyone dare to look askance at her.' It sounds like Hitler on the eve of the Second World War. In fact, these words were used by William II in 1900. So even at that time we see Germany heading for extremes, for a brutal, banal Realpolitik: no political imagination, no moral principles – nothing but power politics and ambition. Germany had become a nation without a guiding ideal, without a spiritual objective.

Prussia had long been dead when the Allied Control Commission decreed her dissolution on 25 February 1947. She died in 1871 when she was absorbed into Germany and the gold rush of the industrial boom took possession of her people. There was only one occasion before her official termination by the occupation forces, that the spirit of Prussia showed itself – to bid a last farewell. That was the attempt on

Hitler's life on 20 July 1944. The list of those executed includes names from every stratum of society and every calling; it also includes the greatest names of Prussian history: Yorck, Moltke, Schwerin, Schulenburg, Lehndorff. Germany's honour was lost; nothing could save it: the disgrace of the Hitler period was too great. But the cross planted on Prussia's grave by those men shines brightly through the darkness of the years.

Thirty years have gone by. There is no Germany any longer, but there are still Germans, even if they are called something else now. And if we ask ourselves: have we today a goal beyond economic ambition and defence policy? Does our state have a *raison d'être*? I believe the answer is yes. Our national egotism has been tamed by the European Economic Community which now has ten members. Our political aim is Europe. And so the standards and values of our society have also changed. This is the first time the Germans have known what it is like to belong to an alliance; the first time they have not had to maintain themselves in isolation.

And we also have a moral objective: the preservation of freedom. The motto is no longer power for power's sake. Instead, we claim just so much external power as we need to defend our liberty; and just so much internal power as we can control. For to imagine that government can do without power and power structures is delusion. To make government tolerable, on the other hand, is a reasonable aim.

The Germans have learnt. They have become more modest in their demands, more critical of themselves and, thank goodness, more tolerant too. They are slightly more considerate towards their neighbours – and towards others in general. They don't talk quite so loud and they are not quite so assertive and self-confident as they once were. The shadow of the past has taught them to understand many things they did not understand before.

13

2

From Collapse to Re-creation

The Federal Republic, founded in 1949, occupies the geographical position represented by East Prussia for many centuries: it is the eastern frontier zone of the western world. That this would happen could not immediately have been foreseen when the war ended in May 1945. When 12 million refugees from the east were streaming into the ravaged territories west of the Elbe, into cities transformed into immense fields of rubble by innumerable bombing attacks, no one dreamed of a Federal Republic or a GDR.

In June 1946 at Potsdam the Allies had decided to divide Germany into occupation zones and to administer the whole country through a Control Commission. No one – including the victors with their alliance already beginning to crumble – had any precise idea of how this would happen or what was to happen next.

In the spring of 1945 I too was a refugee fleeing from east to west. But I could not possibly transmit to anyone today what I experienced and what I felt then. So I shall go back to something I wrote at the time. I had just become a journalist and this was my first piece for *Die Zeit*. The date is 20 March 1946, and the title: 'The Ride to the West – With the Tide of Refugees'.

> 20 March 1946. My notebook says 'Arrival in V'. It is a year now since I arrived in a little place called Vinsebeck in Westphalia. I was going to leave my faithful horse at the Metternich

stud after it had carried me loyally all the way from East Prussia to the West.

We set out together on 21 January 1945. It was late in the evening. An order to evacuate – soon overtaken by events – and the noise of battle getting closer all the time had alarmed us. On all the farms around people were hurriedly packing their carts in the dark, opening their barn doors, and untying their cattle. It all happened as in a dream and only took a few hours. And then the great exodus began from the promised land of home – though not, as in Abraham's day, with the covenant of a 'land I will show you' – but out into the night with no goal and no leader.

They converged from all the villages and all the roads: wagons, horses, people with handcarts, hundreds, thousands; from north and south they streamed incessantly on to the main east–west road and crawled slowly on, day after day, as though the horses' pace were the measure of every hour and of all time.

With the sky full of planes, the thunder of guns, the noise of armoured convoys passing us, we ploughed on, step by step, through the icy snow storms of the east. We spent the nights around camp fires on the road or else in the barns of abandoned farmyards; every dawn brought the same scene: dying children and old people closing their eyes which reflected the fear and anxiety and suffering of generations.

Week after week went by. The war raged behind us like an angry sea, and before us the carts stretched endlessly into the distance. Is it the flight from Egypt, is it something from the migrations in the Dark Ages, is it an immense river of people streaming westwards, growing longer and longer? 'Brother, take thy brethren with thee.' As the river rolls through countries and provinces, more and more streams of carts and people flow into it.

The orphaned villages remain behind, in Pomerania, in Brandenburg, in Mecklenburg, and the train is still growing, the chain getting longer. For a long time now two or three carts have been travelling abreast, blocking the whole breadth of the road. But it doesn't matter; they are all going the same way – no one wants to drive east. Only our thoughts go back there every day, all these homeless thoughts and dreams. No one speaks. There are no tears. The only sound is the grinding of the wheels as they gradually run out of grease.

Many milestones of eastern history line the endless road: the Teutonic knights of Marienburg, Bismarck's property at Varzin, Hitler's fortress at Kolberg. We crossed the Nogat, the Vistula, the Oder, and the Elbe. Gradually snow and ice melt away; as we travel through Schaumburg spring is breaking into flower. Gradually the stream of wandering refugees has ebbed away and flowed into new harbours and cramped ports.

By the time I cross the Weser bridge at Rinteln on my bay I am quite alone. We ride past Barntrup, a little town with a pretty renaissance castle rising from the centre. I see a wooded range of hills before me: soon somewhere behind it I shall find the goal of my long journey's end. The road snakes like a slalom track, up through the hanging beech forests already showing a faint glimmer of green. We climb slowly. It is a beautiful day in early spring. The thrushes sing, and a gentle breeze drives the clouds across the warm spring sun.

Suddenly, as we enter the last bend, a solitary figure comes into view on the ridge like a statue against the pale sky: an old man, grey, starving and in rags. His last possessions are in a sack on his back. He holds a stick, and stands, an ageless memorial, his eyes gazing abstractedly into the distant blue of the valley. I do not dare disturb him; I greet him as one greets a wayside cross, with reverence not expecting a reply.

And then the unimaginable happens: coming up the mountain towards us we see many others like the old man; sometimes they walk in twos and threes, sharing the experience of the road; but most of them are alone. The war has taken not only their possessions and their shelter from them, but also the comforting companionship of those they know. Their faces are grey, suffering, and worn, their eyes filled with despair: they are fleeing from the British and the Americans who have occupied the Ruhr.

Is this still Germany, this little corner of the earth where east and west meet, with no home and nowhere to go, like wild animals running from the hunt? Is this the thousand year Reich? A few beggars on a mountain ridge? Is that all that remains of a people who set out to capture the flesh-pots of Europe? The answer is clear: 'Wir haben hier keine Heimat aber die zukünftige suchen wir'. (We have no homeland here but are looking for one.)

Millions like me were wandering aimlessly along the roads

of what would later be called the Federal Republic of Germany. But before that could happen there was much despair, confusion, and especially much fear to be endured. Today it is impossible to imagine how powerful the threat from the east felt to us then. Many people only halted briefly before moving on to Australia, South America, or Canada. They were afraid the Russians would go on advancing: 'If they come, it will take them just twenty-four hours to reach the Atlantic.'

Most people were numbed by the shock of the Russian capture of Berlin with all the atrocities that went with it. And up to 1949 Soviet expansion seemed unstoppable. Few people remember that almost the whole of Eastern Europe fell under Russian domination only *after* the Second World War. In Poland Mikolajezyk, chairman of the Polish Peasant Party and deputy prime minister, and a champion of the Western powers, was forced to flee to the West only in 1947. In Romania it was only in December 1947 that King Michael was made to abdicate. And in Czechoslovakia the *coup* to establish the communist regime did not take place until March 1948. In those days everyone trembled before the communists. Millions of Germans had fled before them, millions more had been driven out and thousands of prisoners of war were kept in labour camps in the Soviet Union until 1955. It was not for nothing that anti-communism struck deep roots in the Federal Republic.

The overriding problem of course was how to forge a better society from the all-prevailing chaos. But there was also another question: how could the criminal regime be liquidated, how could the culprits be discovered and brought to book? For crime must be expiated. This question was of supreme importance, because the only way to establish a new rule of law in Germany and to purge her corrupt and perverted conception of legality was to assess each crime correctly and punish it in exact accordance with its gravity.

When the victors, regarded as conquerors by some and by

17

others as liberators, marched into Germany it was thought that their tribunals would include lawyers from neutral countries to sentence those who had personally committed crimes on the statute book. But that was not to be. The victors set up courts in which they themselves were both judge and prosecutor. They did not measure crime according to existing laws, but instituted new ones, and they did not assess the guilt of individuals, but proclaimed categories of potential criminals such as staff-officers, and automatically arrested them. The result was that victims and opponents of the Nazi regime found themselves sitting side by side with its lackeys on the benches for the accused.

In those days I was very involved with these problems which perturbed everyone and dominated general discussion for years. Two of my articles provide a clear illustration of the problems as they presented themselves. The first was called 'Six Members of the Master Race' and appeared in *Die Zeit* on 8 July 1954.

At Metz, six of the accused commandants and officers from the concentration camp at Struthof (near Strasbourg) have been condemned to death. During the trial one of the six rose to his feet one day and said: 'If my death could help to appease the general hatred of the Germans, I should be glad to die.' The president of the tribunal replied: 'You are not being tried because you are a German. You are being tried because you are a criminal. Don't try and delude yourself and others that this action is being brought against Germany.' It is true that the crimes before the Metz tribunal were so repulsive that they seemed like long distance photographs of horrifying creatures on a remote planet: no one could have wished to be identified with them.

There was a long procession of witnesses at Metz: Germans, Frenchmen, Norwegians, and Belgians. Each man told a slight variant of the same tale of painful lives and deaths. Only the actual causes of death differed slightly: there was starvation (nine-tenths of the inmates died of deprivation; one-tenth were put to death); they were shot in the back of the neck, taken to the gas chamber, or hanged, either from a gallows or from a big meat hook in the crematorium which, when 'fully functional', belched out huge flames. For 'practical reasons' these energy sources were attached to the hot water system: when enough people had been killed there were hot showers. Life and death in a concentration camp differ only in posing different technical problems.

Most of the accused are primitive types who received their first education and training in the Death's Head Units of the ss. Some of them had known nothing but the camp atmosphere from 1933-4 onwards, serving first as guards, and then as commandants. Some, it turned out, had spent the whole war without firing a shot except to despatch one of their victims. They had learnt to live and to think only in accordance with the concepts of the concentration camp. They recognized only two categories of human beings: the master race and 'inferior' persons who had to be exterminated. Over the years they came to regard the camp inmates as a butcher regards an animal: he does not 'feel' he is killing.

One of the accused had taught his seven-year-old son to throw stones at the columns of prisoners, in order to train him not to think of them as human beings. When the mood seized him, this same man would tear off one of the prisoner's cap and throw it a long way; then he would order the man to fetch it; as the prisoners were not allowed to leave their columns this counted as an escape bid and the guard was therefore 'under orders' to shoot the prisoner: which he did.

People like the six accused and forty-three others who were condemned to death *in absentia* have probably existed at all times. But for such potential criminals not merely to become actual criminals, as occasion may arise, but to be appointed as leaders of a so-called élite and given unlimited power – that can only happen under a totalitarian regime which sets up its own *Weltanschauung* in place of eternally valid laws. As soon as these are abandoned, strange ideas will arise as to what is worth living for or dying for.

The accused kept pointing out that they were acting on orders, and that they themselves would have been shot if they had not complied with commands to murder, beat, and torture. Maybe. But is it really so much easier to die at Stalingrad – as doubtless every one of them would uncomplainingly have done had he been sent to the front – than to lay down one's life in order not to commit a crime?

19

The other piece appeared in *Die Zeit* on 29 December 1949; it was about General von Falkenhausen, an honorable man who not only did nothing wrong, but on the contrary prevented many injustices. Yet he was charged and tried because as a military commander he fell into the category of 'members of the leadership'.

For months a lonely old man has been sitting in the courtroom in Brussels. Silently and absently he stares at the procession of accusers filing past: it is Alexander von Falkenhausen, the former military commander of Belgium. And this is how the Belgian defence lawyer, Monsieur Botson, has just concluded his plea: 'It is not the place of this court to pass justice on Germany or the Third Reich, but on Falkenhausen; he bears no sort of moral responsibility for the horrors of the Nazi regime to which he was politically opposed; and there is no doubt that he did everything in his power to prevent some of its outrages.'

Falkenhausen is one of the few Germans who were bitterly opposed to Hitler as early as 1933, when many of the others who later joined the resistance were still taking part in the Potsdam celebrations with feelings of awe and reverence. He began to voice his warnings from 1930 onwards in speeches delivered in the Dresden area. In August 1932 he tried in vain to persuade General von Schleicher, then minister of defence, to outlaw the SA. After the Harzburger Front (the union of the Nazis with the right-wing parties) was established, he left the German National Party; a little later, when Seldte amalgamated the Stahlhelm with the SA, he resigned from that also.

He finally seized his chance when Marshal Chiang Kai-shek invited him to China. Disappointed and disgusted with the turn of events in Germany, he sailed for China in April 1934 – just in time to avoid the fate of his brother who was murdered on the notorious 30 June 1934. But his freedom did not last long. In 1938 Ribbentrop forced him to return by threatening to arrest his family: after the pact between Germany and Japan Germans were no longer allowed to serve as private military advisers in China.

Falkenhausen was recalled to the army in 1938, and in May 1940 a number of influential and responsible officers arranged for him to be sent to Belgium as military commandant – much against his will. In this period he waged a constant battle with the Party, the security services (SD), and the police. In December 1943 the Gestapo arrested the commandant of the Brussels prisons. They said he had committed 'treason' by reporting abuses against the prisoners to the military commandant, who intervened strongly on their behalf. Falkenhausen's efforts to prevent forced labour in Belgium culminated in his refusal to call up those born in 1925, with the result that on 14 July he was relieved of his post.

After that he spent nine months being dragged through various concentration camps and prisons by the Gestapo. In spite of that he was arrested as a war criminal shortly after the liberation. That was nearly five years ago. Falkenhausen has now been in fifty-one prisons and camps in six different countries; while his successor, the former Gauleiter of Cologne-Aix, Grohé, whose regime as Commissioner in Belgium was considerably more severe, was sentenced to prison there but has long since been released.

Perhaps in some more humane age the story will be told of the *chevalier sans peur et sans reproche* who perished in prison because people had forgotten the difference between good and evil.

The curse of the totalitarian states where only categories count and individuals do not matter seemed to have fallen on the liquidators of the system too. For instance, all the members of the General Staff were interned as potential criminals, although the vast majority had nothing to answer for.

The most absurd case I ever came across was that of Arthur Dietzsch. In 1923, when he was a twenty-three-year-old officer in the Reichswehr, he was condemned to ten years' confinement in a fortress because he was supposed to have taken an active part in communist meetings, which was illegal at the time. (He was engaged to the daughter of an old member of the Communist Party.) He had just served his ten years when the Nazis came to power. 'A communist? Off with him to a concentration camp.' So there he sat out the next thirteen years until the end of the Thousand Year Reich. But even then the day of liberation had not dawned for him. In the concentration camp he had been forced to take part in

21

experiments on spotted fever. Because of this an American special court condemned him to fifteen years' imprisonment, although there was no doubt that his case was one of duress, and that there was evidence that Dietzsch had managed to save the lives of several prisoners. It was only after 1950, when he had been in prison from the age of twenty-three to fifty, that he was released as a result of several articles in *Die Zeit*.

When the Allies set about ending the Hitler regime after the capitulation, their jurisdiction was governed by two ideas: one was that it was possible and necessary to prevent war for ever after; the other was that National Socialism had only been able to spread because individuals had not put up sufficient resistance. They forgot that heroism is a very rare quality and cannot be set up as a norm. Every proceeding of the Allied courts after 1945 was based on the accusation that the Germans had offered no resistance to the regime. So the age-old question of whether the citizen has a right to revolt against authority was turned into the assertion that it is his duty to do so – in complete opposition to what St Paul says in his *Epistle to the Romans*.

Nobody can be surprised if the Allied special tribunals in the various zones of occupation sometimes delivered judgements, especially during the early days, which cannot be considered just by normal standards. After all, they were confronted with crimes which had hitherto been unimaginable in the civilized world.

In 1945 almost every German was prepared to do his utmost to bring the criminals to justice for their horrendous crimes, which had only just become general knowledge. But after a few years it was not unknown for people to feel a certain amount of satisfaction if they heard that one of the internees had escaped. Why was this? Because the idea had begun to spread that the Allies were misusing the tribunals to get rid of groups and individuals whom, for some reason or other, they found troublesome. Thus people whom public opinion had never identified with the worst aspects of the system, such as industrialists, ministers, and generals, were branded as the chief culprits and arraigned before the Nuremberg court.

After that there were years of German tribunals whose duty it was to carry out the de-Nazification policy and who created further confusion. Helene Schwärzel, for instance, was condemned to fifteen years' penitentiary. She was the member of the Hitler Youth who had denounced Goerdeler, a leader of the resistance movement, and more or less innocently pocketed the reward for doing so, which had been offered by the Nazis who regarded him as guilty of high treason. She received the same sentence as the leaders of the special groups who had been found guilty of torture and mass murder.

No wonder, when too many were accused, that too many were defended. The confusion in the way the law was administered created doubt. Because the innocent and the guilty were condemned equally, public opinion moved towards the other extreme: the eventual conclusion was that apart from Hitler everyone was really more or less innocent, and that the Allied sentences should not be taken seriously. This is another reason why – as is so often claimed – we have not yet come to terms with the past.

In spite of the chaotic and depressing circumstances most people remember the years 1945–6 with a certain amount of nostalgia. Many feel that never before or after have they lived their lives so intensely. The external circumstances are now forgotten: a landscape of ruins as far as the eye could see, no transport, hardly any food, not enough fuel – if you wanted to read you did so in bed with gloves on and a shawl round your shoulders. All that remains are the memories of discussions going on all through the night, of unexpected encounters and of the first books coming in from outside.

All our thoughts and discussions in those days were about spiritual and political revival. What should the new Germany be like? What must we do? What should be our goals? Centralism or federalism? What kind of a constitution? What priorities for reconstruction? Educational reforms – but how? The questions were innumerable and our interest in where we should go and what standards we should adopt knew no bounds. Material things seemed trivial by comparison: they were unattainably far and not so important anyhow. All our energy was concentrated on spiritual, moral, and political necessities.

Amazingly soon, in the winter of 1945–6, new publications began to appear all over the country, including *Die Sammlung* in Göttingen, published by two educationalists, Wilhelm Flitner and Hermann Nohl; *Die Wandlung* in Heidelberg; *Die Gegenwart* in Freiburg, where Benno Reifenberg and Robert Härdter were the heirs of the old *Frankfurter Zeitung*; *Der Aufbau*, in Berlin, where early editors included Heinrich Mann and Georg Lukács; *Der Ruf*, in Munich, originally the paper of the German POWs in the USA; and *Frankfurter Hefte* in Frankfurt. Of all these publications *Die Wandlung* was probably the most important because the publishers, the philosopher Karl Jaspers and the sociologist Alfred Weber, represented great attractions. An important group had collected around them in Heidelberg. Discussions lasting several days were arranged there, and in spite of all the difficulties of transport, they were attended from the very beginning by Carlo Schmidt, Adolf Arndt, and Heinrich von Brentano.

After the long years of intellectual drought everyone was thirsty. Conditions were as they had been after the destruction of Pompeii: there were no books, no paper, only a few people, and it was a long time until one was able to discover who was still living and, particularly, where they were living. It was with real excitement that people opened the first issue of a cultural, political or literary magazine. And it was a great event when *Die Wandlung* first appeared, containing excerpts from Alfred Weber's book *Farewell to History*, and a preface by Karl Jaspers, the great warning mentor of the Germans.

In his book *Zwischen Freiheit und Quarantäne* ('Between Freedom and Quarantine') Hans-Werner Richter has captured something of what people sometimes described as 'the blessing of zero hour' – i.e. the chance of recreating the world: 'Germany, it was thought, stood at a decisive turning-point in her history. Many possibilities lay before her. She had to fight her way from "non-existence" to a totally new existence. She could fix her own goals according to her geographical position and her political possibilities. She could become more modern, more in accordance with the times, and acquire more faith in the future than any other nation.'[4] Whether she succeeded or not must be left for others to decide.

3

Konrad Adenauer

Konrad Adenauer's roots go far back into the nineteenth century. He was born when Bismarck was at the height of his power; Ulysses Grant, the victorious commander-in-chief of the Union forces in the Civil War was still President of the United States; and in England Disraeli had just spent £4 million on the packet of Suez Canal shares that the Khedive Ismail had been forced to sell. Adenauer was already thirty-eight years old when the First World War broke out: his political ideas and his view of the world were formed in the period before 1914 – a period when Europe was still the centre of the world and the hereditary enmity between France and Germany her greatest problem.

Konrad Adenauer was the son of a low-ranking civil servant. In 1917 he became Chief Burgomaster of Cologne, one of the oldest and most distinguished cities in Germany. He wrote of it with pride and affection: 'Holy Cologne, founded by the Romans, formed by Christian values, developing in the spirit of humanism – in the high Middle Ages she was the heart of Europe.' Konrad Adenauer, the head of this city, was the German chief burgomaster best known abroad, and at home he was the most powerful man in local politics. At the same time he was President of the Prussian State Council which had been founded in 1919 as a sort of second Chamber; and on top of all that he had a deciding voice in the Centre Party.

In 1926 Adenauer was offered the German Chancellorship but he refused it. His authorized biographer Paul Weymar reproduces Adenauer's notes on the negotiations that took

place in Berlin in 1926.[5] They show that he made his acceptance conditional on a broad coalition, because he wanted to
be sure of always having a majority at his disposal. He did
not wish to become the victim of the party dissensions that
were a feature of the period. After all, the Weimar Republic
had already had twelve governments in the seven years of its
existence. In those days it was easy to collect a majority for
a vote of no confidence, and to topple the Chancellor and
his cabinet. Hence, when formulating the Constitution of
the Federal Republic in 1948, the Parliamentarian Council
stipulated that 'The Chancellor can only be removed if a
majority in the Federal Assembly agrees on a successor'.

In 1926 the broad coalition could not be guaranteed, and
so it was with relief that Adenauer returned to his native city.
Immediately after the Nazis came to power in 1933 he was
deposed; for a while he was spitefully persecuted, and once
he was arrested; but for the most part he lived as a private
citizen in Rhöndorf near Bonn. At that time no one would
have thought it possible that after the 'Thousand Year Reich'
he would be recalled to higher tasks and greater responsibili-
ties.

Konrad Adenauer was seventy-three when he became
Chancellor of the Federal Republic in 1949. He led his country for fourteen years and had a more decisive hand in mould-
ing it than any other man. Adenauer was totally unpreten-
tious, but decidedly authoritarian. He was self-confident by
nature, but modest as well. He had no personal ambition, but
he wanted power because he was convinced that he, and he
alone, would be able to lead the Germans back to the right
path. A master of tactics, he used much craft and guile to gain
power. At last he got it – not for his own pleasure but for the
good of his people – and even when he had held it long
enough, he still hung on.

Churchill once said that apart from Bismarck, Adenauer
was the greatest head of government Germany had ever had.
The historian Golo Mann, son of Thomas Mann, made this
comparison the subject of an essay:

Both men had great confidence in themselves and not much confidence in the German people. But Bismarck was an artiste, a reckless gambler who could juggle with many balls at once. Adenauer firmly held a single ball in his hands and carried it – always in the same direction. Bismarck had a feudal, historical way of thinking: he thought in concepts like the state, class, domination, power, superpower – all of which had already become anachronisms by the time he was old. Adenauer thought in terms of society, and the only reason he wanted to pursue a great German foreign policy was in order to abolish great German foreign policy for ever. Bismarck was a brilliant, witty writer and an intellectual adventurer – Adenauer was not. Bismarck was a *Junker*, privileged and audacious by birth; Adenauer was a hard-working citizen. . . . There were, however, also similarities arising from their profession, and especially from the German tradition in that profession. Both were avid for power; first, because they wanted to accomplish great things with it; and later because they had become too thoroughly used to it, because they had begun to feel that they themselves were indispensable institutions, and because not to have power had become unthinkable. Both were wily tacticians in small matters; and in great ones they combined consistency, honesty, and loyalty with the exact opposites . . .

Neither of them had much time for ideas. They dealt with concrete matters on a day-to-day basis – an attitude that attracts success, but also carries dangers with it. Each of them had built up a myth of his own personal success, and each had become the dupe of that myth – which faded as the end approached. Both were religious and had a sense of duty, and both were upright men precisely because of their sense of duty. But religion and politics were not the same thing. Strong characters both, they surrounded themselves with men of a lower moral calibre: this was because their intolerance and distrust made them always ready to equate other people's independent opinions with stupidity or bad intentions.[6]

Compared with Bismarck, Adenauer was indeed a simplifier. He often said that politics should be simple. Once Günter Gaus asked him during a broadcast whether being called a great simplifier struck him as praise or blame, and he replied,

'I consider it very great praise. For, indeed, one should see things so profoundly that they become simple. If you only look at the surface, things are not simple; but if you look into the depths, then you see what is real, and that is always simple.'[7]

Adenauer thought in alternatives. He saw things in terms of either/or: a social market economy or planning; freedom or slavery. He was the ideal leader for the period of the Cold War; tough, imperturbable, and concentrated on a few very important things; all else he called 'undergrowth and ballast'. He had a natural feeling for what was possible and wasted no time on analysis and fruitless considerations – he relied on his instinct, seized every opportunity by the forelock, and acted. Intellectual matters were foreign to him.

Konrad Adenauer believed that it was better for the press – and for the public as well – to meddle as little as possible with politics, especially with foreign policy. Therefore he did not think much of regular press conferences; but he liked giving interviews. As he was very keen on secrecy his press officers had a hard time – none of the first four lasted more than a few months.

Arnulf Baring writes, 'No politician could keep afloat in the Chancellor's entourage unless he had decided to unite his fate absolutely with Adenauer's and was ready to give up all political independence. The Federal Chancellor needed advisers and assistants – but he alone must lead. He himself decided policy, especially foreign policy.'[8]

Herbert Blankenhorn probably knew him more intimately than anyone else. He worked with him for many years, as Secretary-General of the CDU and then as Adenauer's liaison officer to the Allied Control Commission. He writes: 'Adenauer's relations with his ministers and the important men in his party were matter of fact and cool, often critical. He was not displeased to see important figures at loggerheads. Nor did he refrain from denigratory opinions about people whose growing influence annoyed him. He did not enjoy thinking about his successor and only did it from time to time under pressure of public opinion or of certain party groupings. He did not act as a "crystallizer", that is to say he did not surround himself with talented younger politicians and allow them to share his ideas and aims so that they could develop into pillars of his policy.'[9]

Adenauer would never have thought it possible for the SPD to rule the country. He regarded the Social Democrats as basically a Prussian party. In his view their leaders were the heirs of the Prussian Junkers, 'They have exactly the same desire to dominate, only with them it is in economics and politics and not in military affairs.'

In September 1954, after the collapse of the European Defence Community which he favoured, he made some remarks to the Belgian Foreign Secretary, Henri Spaak and his Luxembourg colleague, Joseph Bech, and it is hard to know whether he was thinking of the 'Sozis'. Lothar Ruehl, today deputy government speaker, who was then working for *Der Spiegel*, unintentionally overheard this conversation without being noticed by the three politicians, and he reported it verbatim: 'I do not know what will become of Germany when I am no longer there, unless we succeed in creating Europe first ... Do make the most of my lifetime. When I am gone it will be too late. My God, I don't know what my successors will do if they are left to themselves without a clearly demarcated path to follow, and if they are not bound to Europe ...'

Konrad Adenauer was a reserved, matter-of-fact man. His speeches were wooden, his memoirs which he began to write at the age of eighty-eight are so dry that even his warmest supporter cannot enjoy reading them, especially as he refrained from any kind of humour – the quality which distinguished him and for which he was famous. All his life he was a master of witty repartee. Often in his parliamentary career he succeeded in drowning disagreeable interruptions or irritating questions in a tide of laughter. But none of his speeches was a brilliant rhetorical masterpiece. As one of his opponents, Kurt Schumacher, the leader of the SPD, once said,

'Goethe had a vocabulary of 29,000 words; Herr Adenauer only has 200 at his disposal.' 'And even if he knew another 200 words,' said a colleague, 'he wouldn't use them. That's precisely his strong point.'

Another strong point was his exceptional nose for opportunities and public moods. Once he had chosen a course he pursued it with imperturbable consistency. For this reason I am astonished by the spontaneity expressed in a story I was told by Nahum Goldmann, for many years the President of the Jewish World Congress. Adenauer was going to Rome for his first audience with the Pope. The visit had been discussed beforehand in the cabinet, and Adenauer had had to promise that he would not kneel, but as Adenauer put it, 'When the door opened and I suddenly found myself face to face with the Holy Father, I sank to my knees . . .' Goldmann saw a lot of Adenauer and has reported some interesting conversations with him. One was a dispute as to which was greater, Palestrina or Bach. Adenauer's verdict was: 'Palestrina – Bach is too Protestant for my liking.' They also argued about St Francis of Assisi versus St Ignatius of Loyola. Goldmann loved St Francis best, but Adenauer was in favour of Ignatius because, 'He had to fight to win his faith, and he subdued the Self.'

The Adenauer period lasted as long as the Weimar Republic and longer than Hitler's Germany. Its concrete achievements, as opposed to its style, will endure (unlike those of the two preceding eras) because of Adenauer's three important contributions to the future of Germany: the integration of the Federal Republic into the free world; her reconciliation with France; and the foundation of a party uniting the two religions – Roman Catholicism and Protestantism – that had been enemies for centuries.

But the chapter of German history written by Adenauer is not all of a piece. It falls into two parts. In the first we see a man of unfailingly certain intuition, of great persistence, and calm dignity gradually winning back the trust of the rest of the world for the German people who had become a nation of murderers in the eyes of all the others. He did this without ever making unreasonable demands; he never allowed himself to be involved in argument, but simply relied on the natural course of things to give the Germans back their rights. Patiently, and eventually with success, he laboured to end the various restrictions, demolition orders, and forced shipments, yet he never resorted to nationalistic arguments. With imperturbable dedication he gave back to the Germans their sense of direction, proportion, and measure at a time when the greatest catastrophe in their history had confused and disillusioned them to a point where they were entirely governed by despair, helplessness and fear.

In the second phase those very qualities which had made him so effective in the first contributed to his downfall. His certainty of being on the right course and his unshakeable determination to remain on it turned into lack of political imagination, barren obstinacy, and an irritable contempt for his fellow citizens. He was not interested in the views or warnings of atomic scientists, independent politicians, or independent publicists.

It is difficult to draw the line between these two phases. In his foreign policy, it was clear from the 1950s onwards that the fear of taking risks was driving him into the arms of so-called well-tried principles: so that with the risks he also eliminated all opportunities. And yet it was obvious after Stalin's death in 1953 and after the Twentieth Party Congress in 1956 which shook the Eastern bloc to its foundations, that the position of the Soviet Union could not be the same as before.

It must be added, though, that from the very beginning Adenauer spoke with two voices. To the Germans he never tired of dwelling on the reunification of a free and peaceful Germany, and the right of the Federal Republic to speak for the whole nation; but when addressing the world at large he made it clear that he regarded the integration of the Federal Republic into the West as the most important issue of all, even if his opponents thought that this might confirm the division of Germany for all time.

At the beginning the Iron Curtain protected the Federal Republic against Communist infiltration; but from 1953 onwards – and the uprising of 17 June offers the clearest evidence of this – it was the other side who felt the need for protection: the East began to be afraid of infiltration by Western notions of freedom. Bonn, however, did not seem to notice this change. In spite of admonitions from all the other Western countries, the Federal government went on anxiously avoiding all contact with 'the other side', and thereby saved the other side a number of embarrassments.

And this at a time when it might perhaps have been possible for the FDR to alter the course of her policy not only towards the Soviet Union but also towards other members of the Eastern bloc. With their revolution of October 1956 the Poles tried – not without some success – to shake off direct domination by the USSR; they showed themselves astonishingly ready to meet representatives of the Federal Republic; and in 1957 the Polish Premier Rapacki, speaking at a Plenary Session of the United Nations, advocated the ban of atomic weapons from Europe. If at that moment the FDR had decided on a more active Eastern policy we might not have continued to be suspected of militarism, revisionism, and a policy of revenge for another fifteen years. Indeed, we could have acted far more constructively.

Konrad Adenauer's political rise began on 1 September 1948, the date of his election to the Council of the Assembly (*Parlamentarischer Rat.*). It was the task of the Council to work out the constitution. This was the first institution to encompass the whole Federal Republic; until then there had been no President and no Assembly, only the governments of the individual *Länder*. Adenauer seized his opportunity and immediately got the Allies to agree that only the Council of the Assembly, namely Adenauer himself, was to negotiate with them, and not the Conference of Prime Ministers.

The first elections to the Federal Assembly were held on 14 August 1949. There were 402 seats. The Conservatives, the CDU/CSU, won 139, and the Social Democrats, the SPD, 131. So the two big parties were of more or less equal strength. The question therefore arose: should the foundations of the new state be laid by a coalition of all parties, or by a coalition of the Right, a middle-class bloc? Adenauer was in no doubt. He did not want to share his power nor have his view of the world diluted. Until the end of his days he believed that this was the most important political decision of his life.

A few months later a wrangle that had been going on for weeks was brought to a close: the question was whether the government should be in Frankfurt or in Bonn. On 3 November the Federal Assembly voted in favour of Bonn by 200 votes to 179. Herbert Blankenhorn noted in his diary, 'As so often happens in history: important decisions are made for personal reasons. Although Adenauer never said so, the fact that his official headquarters would be near his house at Rhöndorf and easily accessible was quite decisive.'[10]

It is hard to say whether Adenauer had a masterplan for the future or whether, and this is my view, he took decisions on a day-to-day basis, a process which led to what he considered the best possible results for the country: integration into the West, rearmament, and the Common Market. But first of all he had to take hold of the reins. Adenauer was an experienced local politician, and he knew how to do it.

In those early days the CDU/CSU was not yet organized on a Federal basis. Adenauer was only the Chairman of the CDU in the British zone of occupation; so no one was entitled to make decisions for the party as a whole. Under the circumstances it was not easy for Adenauer to make himself head of the whole party. It is interesting to observe how he set about it. On 21 August 1949 he invited members of the CDU/CSU to a meeting at Rhöndorf. Adenauer's friend, the banker Robert Pferdmenges, told later how the vital question never arose as to who was to preside, because Adenauer with his usual

cunning and tactical forethought had arranged for the meeting to be held in his own house. So, as he was the host, it was
natural for him to take the chair; and it was he who spoke first
and unfolded his views on the matters under discussion.

By the evening, after a long and heated debate, everyone
was at last ready to agree with the host that a small coalition
with Adenauer as Federal Chancellor would be best. It was
also decided straight away to offer the Presidency to Theodor
Heuss, the Chairman of the FDP, who had not even heard
what was going on. This was done on 12 September 1949,
and three days later Adenauer was elected Federal Chancellor
with a majority of one vote – his own.

When Adenauer became Chancellor the supreme power
lay in the hands of the three Occupying Powers, personified
by their three high commissioners. They had the right to veto
any new laws that were promulgated, and they also retained
their hold over Germany's foreign policy. All important
questions had to be negotiated between the high commissioners and Adenauer, and he was very careful to see that he
alone and not the departmental ministers, attended the thrice-
weekly meetings on the Petersberg. His right to be the sole
representative of the Federal Republic at these meetings gave
the Chancellor a unique opportunity to consolidate his position. In the first few years he succeeded in concentrating all
the most important functions of the executive in the office of
the Chancellor. Long before the Germans were allowed to
manage their own foreign affairs, defence or information
services, the Chancellor's office contained various sections
where preparations were going ahead to set up these ministries when the time came: not only were their functions being
planned, but also their personnel.

This structure had the great advantage for Adenauer that
he did not need to discuss anything with his departmental
ministers, but could take decisions on his own. He never had
it so good again as in those first years when the constitution
was being drafted: he could use the Allies as an excuse for
whatever measures he saw fit to take; the Assembly had not

yet grown rebellious; his party, which had only been organized on a Federal basis since October 1950, was still without much influence; and the views of the Opposition did not bother him for he felt certain that he alone possessed the true doctrine.

Arnulf Baring writes:

The initial opportunity for the first head of the Federal Government lay in monopolizing all foreign policy matters inside the Office of the Federal Chancellor – an Office staffed with highly qualified officials, screened off from the influence of the parties and the unions, and controlled solely by the Chancellor himself. Entirely shut off from party politics, it was the one centre for decision-making, containing, as it did, the administration for Foreign Affairs which was later to become the Foreign Office; the 'Blank' Office, a forerunner of the Ministry of Defence; and also the information service of the Federal Press Office which had been specially tailored to suit the needs of the Chancellor.

Even Konrad Adenauer's own support system, the Federal President, the government, and the majority party in the Assembly, as well as all the big unions were almost entirely excluded from the decision-making process in foreign affairs. The Opposition and a vaguely apprehended public opinion counted for even less. The three high commissioners, on the other hand, were important: in the early days their wishes were decisive. In collaboration with them and their governments the Federal Chancellor was able to initiate his foreign policy of rearmament and integration into the West within a sort of party political vacuum.[11]

I quote again from the interview with Günter Gaus:

Gaus: As a Federal Chancellor did you always feel safest when you were in a situation where you were the sole decision maker?

Adenauer: If I found myself in a position where I alone had to make a decision, and I was convinced that I had all the necessary evidence before me, then I felt very calm about taking that decision on my own.

Gaus: And you never felt it a burden to have to make decisions?

Adenauer: No.

That is the only question in the interview that the Chancellor answered with a single word.[12]

When Adenauer chose people for various departments the first thing he demanded was absolute loyalty; more even: he demanded devotion. He had no use for independent characters with their own ideas and the ability to get their own way. He mistrusted such people – unless he happened to know their secret weaknesses and could therefore be sure of being able to use his knowledge as a weapon should necessity arise. Another part of his repertoire of political tactics was to play off one adviser against another. Everyone who worked closely with Adenauer or included him in his memoirs has spoken with admiration of his practical achievements, but no one praises his human qualities. He had no illusions, little heart, and a dry, sly, sometimes aggressive sense of humour. He was cunning, sceptical, occasionally ruthless, and he knew all the tricks and manœuvres of a hard-boiled politician.

But he was an impressive personality with great natural authority. He combined amenability and scepticism, toughness and the readiness to compromise, tenacity and flexibility in an inimitable fashion. He would put up with theoretical analysis and lengthy discussion only if they seemed to him essential for taking practical action. He wanted to see order and prosperity restored in Germany, and hard work and efficiency rewarded. He was not very interested in leading the people towards moral regeneration. Altogether he was much more positive, generous, and reliable in foreign than in internal affairs. He liked being called a gardener who tends and cultivates his beloved roses, but in the field of home policy he lacked horticultural ability.

Adenauer had a very sharp sense for any potentially dangerous rival; and before he was established as Federal Chancellor there were quite a number of those, particularly the men who had founded the CDU in the most difficult circumstances, in Russian-occupied Berlin – long before the West German CDU came into existence. There were Andreas Hermes, Jakob Kaiser, and Hans Schlange-Schöningen.

Hermes had been Minister for Finance in the Weimar Republic, Schlange-Schöningen Minister for Agriculture, and Kaiser had been a leading trade unionist. All of them should have been indispensable to the building of a new Germany. But Adenauer studiously managed to keep them out of the way until he was definitely settled.

Andreas Hermes mentions this in his diary.[13] Today we cannot imagine the history of the Federal Republic without Adenauer as its architect; but in 1945 nobody thought of this long-forgotten politician – it was men like Andreas Hermes who occupied the foreground, men who had distinguished themselves actively in the fight against Hitler. Hermes had resigned his seat as a Centre Party member in the Reichstag after the fire in February 1933. In March he was arrested for having twice pulled down the swastika which had been hoisted at the headquarters of the Farmers' Union. He was released after six months and emigrated to Colombia. In 1939 he returned to Germany. He was arrested after the attempt on Hitler's life, 20 July 1944, and condemned to death. He was kept in chains night and day in a Berlin prison where he waited for his execution while the Allied bombs gradually reduced the city to rubble.

Immediately after his release in early May 1945 he received a visit from Walter Ulbricht and a Soviet major. Was he prepared to undertake the provisioning of the city which had no water, no electricity, and no food? He accepted without hesitation. Together with those of his friends from the Resistance who were still alive he restored the city's administration. Jakob Kaiser, who had spent nine months hiding from the Gestapo at Babelsberg, tried to unite all the trade unions under one umbrella.

In mid-June the Russians permitted the foundation of political parties. Hermes had been thinking about a new party since the Resistance period. It was to be a non-Marxist, social party based on the two religions. He had worked out the details in prison, and as soon as he was released he discussed them with his friends. On 15 June about thirty of them assembled in his house: they included members of the Catholic and Protestant clergy; Ernst Lemmer was among them, and Walter Schreiber, who for many years had been the Prussian Minister for Commerce and Industry and a member of the former Democratic Party.

The Communists wanted to unite the new parties in an 'anti-Fascist bloc'. Hermes refused and worked out a compromise which was accepted by all, including the Protestant dean Grüber and the Catholic prison chaplain Buchholz. Hermes suggested the name German Democratic Union. Professor von der Gablenz and Professor Dovifat wanted to add 'Christian'. Hermes was against it. Finally they agreed on Christian Democratic Union. Hermes was elected the first Chairman, and Schreiber Deputy Chairman.

On 26 June 1945 the Christian Democratic Union of Germany published a great summons to the German people, signed by Andreas Hermes and thirty-four others, among them Ferdinand Friedensburg, Otto-Heinrich von der Gablenz, Jakob Kaiser, Heinrich Krone, Otto Lenz, Ferdinand Sauerbruch, and Count Yorck von Wartenburg. This was the founding of the CDU. In December a general meeting was called at Godesberg, to which Hermes invited all the newly founded *Länder* and local groups. Adenauer also took part.

Meanwhile the Russians were preparing to introduce land reform in their zone. They were very anxious for the Germans to approve this undertaking. So they tried to bribe Hermes by promising to release his last surviving son who was a prisoner of war in Russia (two others had been killed in the war) if he would agree to the expropriation without compensation of all landowners as part of the land reform.

As the chairman of a party sworn to the principle of private ownership he found himself unable to do this. There was a second conversation, but again he declined because he could not go against his conscience. Thereupon the Russians sent his son, who had already arrived in Potsdam, back to Siberia where he had to spend the next few years. (Today Peter Hermes is the Federal German Ambassador in Washington.)

Wilhelm Külz, on the contrary, the founder of the Liberal Party in the GDR, did what the Russians wanted and signed: his son returned at once.

After his refusal the Russians deposed Andreas Hermes. He left Berlin but continued to canvass the absolute necessity of maintaining relations with the Russians to prevent Germany's Eastern provinces from becoming totally engulfed in their sphere of influence. A few days after Hermes arrived in the West the CDU advisory board for the British zone was to meet at Herford to choose a chairman. Hermes had moved back into his house in Cologne and therefore belonged to the British zone. Even though he had not been expressly invited, as the founder of the Union Hermes thought he would naturally be welcome at Herford, especially as several members wanted to propose him for the chairmanship. When he arrived in Herford he found that Adenauer, as the oldest member present, had taken charge of the meeting. Adenauer forbade Hermes to join the group on the grounds that the Allies had only given permission for certain people to take part. Hermes immediately left Herford. Much later he received a letter from Rhöndorf in which Adenauer expressed his astonishment and distress at hearing that Hermes had left the town.

Adenauer behaved with similar delicacy in a story told to me by someone, who, like Adenauer himself, had been a Centre Party member of the Reichstag before 1939. When he returned to Germany after the war, he paid a visit to Adenauer and told him that Heinrich Brüning had fallen on evil days, and asked whether Adenauer could do something for him; after all, he had been the last important Chancellor of the Weimar days. Adenauer did not write a personal letter to Brüning, as one would have expected, but told Herbert Blankenhorn to send him 1000 marks – which Brüning, of course, indignantly returned. Adenauer was certainly right in not wanting to see Brüning back in German politics; but to have him supervised by the secret police when he was teaching as a professor at Cologne University in order to see who his friends were was taking things rather too far.

There were two important factors in Adenauer's bewildering mentality. The first was resentment against Prussia, a feeling shared by many inhabitants of the Rhineland. It goes back to the days of the Congress of Vienna, where in 1815 Prussia and the Rhineland were welded together – very much to the displeasure of both. 'An old centre of civilization and a colonial country' was the saying at the time, and in 1946 the first Federal Chancellor was still using it as an argument to prevent Berlin from becoming the capital once more. 'We in the West,' he said in an interview with *Die Welt* on 30 November 1946, 'are hostile to much that is usually meant by "the spirit of Prussia". I think it would be better for the German capital to be in the south-west than away in the east in Berlin. The new capital should be in the Main region where Germany's windows open on the West. . . . But if Berlin becomes the new capital, the other nations will never get over their mistrust of Germany. If you make Berlin the new capital, you are creating a new Prussia.'

In his childhood Adenauer had personally experienced the *Kulturkampf* and naturally this had left bitter memories. At that time Bismarck imprisoned Catholic priests and exiled Catholic bishops if they rebelled against the Prussian administration. Adenauer once confessed that in Berlin he always felt himself to be in a heathen city. Arnulf Baring writes that during the Weimar period Adenauer once confidentially remarked that as far as he was concerned the steppes of Asia began at Brunswick; that he always lowered the blinds of his compartment as the train went through Magdeburg and always spat out of the window as it crossed the Elbe. This might be described as Rhenish humour rather than political conviction, but his basic attitude remained anti-Prussian and confirmed his determination that the Federal Republic must face strictly Westwards.

Herbert Blankenhorn says, 'In our conversations he often

mentioned that the new Germany must have its centre of gravity in the south-west. He was convinced that many things in German and European history would have been different if the people of south and west Germany had had more influence in Berlin, because they were more inclined towards compromise and collaboration. The north and east had a great talent for organization and military matters, but they ought to have had a stronger counter-weight from the south and west. He had not shed one tear over Prussia's fall.'[14]

For the sake of simplicity, a quality he rated very highly, everything disagreeable was, for Adenauer, typically Prussian: militarism, nationalism, Marxism, materialism. Moreover, ever since the end of the First World War he had pursued a policy whose aim was to break up Prussia and to combine the western regions of Germany in a 'West German Republic' within the Reich. Karl Dietrich Erdmann has published the protocol of the 'Meeting of the Left Rhine Bank Members of the National Assembly and the Chief Burgomasters of the occupied Rhenish towns' held at Cologne on 1 February 1919 at which Adenauer was Chairman. The object was to convince everyone present that the only way to prevent the annexation of the occupied Left Rhine Bank was for the Germans to anticipate such an event. Adenauer declared 'In my view, ladies and gentlemen, the solution would be for all the Rhine lands – not merely the Left Bank, not merely the Rhine Province, but also the neighbouring regions on the Right Bank – to join together in a West German Federal Republic: a "West German Republic" within the German Reich.'

He went on to paint a picture of how our enemies saw us, and to paint it with so much relish that it is impossible not to conclude that his own views were very similar, especially as he expressly urged his audience to pay heed to the prevailing current of separatism, to the desire to escape from Prussia which was rooted in the innermost soul of the people. He said:

In our enemies' eyes Prussia is the evil spirit of Europe; Prussia is the stronghold of aggressive militarism, the enemy of civilization; Prussia is the country that drove us into war. To make sure that there is no misunderstanding I should like to emphasize that I am describing our opponents' ideas. According to them, Prussia was ruled by a bellicose, ruthless military caste and by the *Junkers*; and Prussia ruled Germany, including west Germany where the native view of life was much more sympathetic to the nations of the *Entente*. If Prussia were divided and the western parts of Germany united in a Federal State known as the 'West German Republic', then Germany could no longer be ruled by the spirit of the east, by a Prussia governed by militarism; the dominance of the circles that ruled Prussia (and therefore Germany) until the Revolution would be eliminated once and for all – even if Prussia were to recover from the Revolution. Because of its size and economic importance the 'West German Republic' would play an important part in the new German Reich, and would therefore be able to influence Germany's foreign policy with its peace-loving attitude.[15]

So after the Second World War Adenauer's long-held political ideas coincided with the prejudices of the Occupying Powers, who also labelled everything unpleasant as 'Prussian'. For them Konrad Adenauer was a guarantee that the Federal Republic would be educated in the right spirit, because for him Europe quite naturally meant only Western Europe. He knew nothing of Northern Europe, he mistrusted the East European states, and the Mediterranean countries were foreign to him. Konrad Adenauer belonged to a generation which did not speak foreign languages and did not travel: he did not see Paris or Rome until he was Federal Chancellor.

What would the future of Germany have been if men like Hermes, Kaiser or Schlange-Schöningen had succeeded in becoming leaders? Men to whom Eastern Germany meant far more than it did to the Prussian-hating Rhinelander Adenauer, who regarded integration into the West as far more important for Germany than reunification? Supposing Andreas Hermes, who founded the CDU, had headed the Federal

Republic; a competent, experienced politician committed to an undivided Germany who would not have accepted the division and who would have fought to keep the country together. Would the FDR and the GDR now be one country? Would they be a neutralized, economically weak hybrid country, neither capitalist nor communist? Or flourishing like Austria? Or would they be an impoverished province on the periphery of the Soviet empire? No one can answer these questions. Hermes would probably have opted for a big coalition, but we do not know whether he would have been able to pursue a completely different policy; nor can it ever be absolutely clear whether there are any circumstances in which the Russians would have permitted 'reunification with freedom'.

We do not know whether policy was not simply pre-ordained by circumstances such as the division of Germany, which was bound to accentuate the differences between the Federal Republic and the East; by the break-up of the wartime Allies, and finally by the increasing rivalry between Moscow and Washington, which gradually turned the Federal Republic into the spearhead of a Western phalanx. In other words, had we so little room for manœuvre that our development could not have been other than it was, whoever held the reins?

History is always the product of natural conditions, the distribution of power, and individual decisions. But there is no norm as to the relative proportions between these three. It is usually hard to determine which factor was decisive; but in our case, in view of Germany's weakness and the absolute power of the victors, it was without question the distribution of power. And that means that neither East nor West would have relaxed their grip on either of the two Germanies.

All the same, opinions can differ about what would have been the best policy. Adenauer and the CDU gave precedence to Germany's alignment with the West and to her integration into it. In the years 1949-55 when the course was being set this led to severe conflicts with the SPD. For the SPD feared that, as the Federal Republic became more involved in Western political, military and economic organizations, the re-unification of Germany would become less and less likely. Thus whenever a new treaty or agreement was made the SPD always insisted that the possibility of negotiating with Moscow should first be explored. Their hope was that instead of integration it might be possible to construct a security system which would satisfy the interests of all the participants, even the Soviet Union.

In later years the CDU, with some justice, would pride itself on its consistent policy while noting with disapproval that the SPD had refused to take part in any important positive decision such as rearmament, membership of NATO, or entry into the Common Market. But people forget that the SPD had quite different ends in view. At that time many Germans, whether they belonged to the SPD or not, kept asking themselves the question: are we not permanently blocking the road to a reunification of Germany by binding ourselves so irrevocably to the West?

The first occasion to ask this question came very early on. Adenauer had only been in office six months when the problem of German rearmament appeared on the horizon, in spite of the fact that the Allies had spent the first years of the Occupation trying to cure the Germans of their militarism and to re-educate them – although Hitler had already done that a great deal more thoroughly. In the very first Petersberg Agreement on 22 November 1949 the Federal government had had to declare its firm intention to 'uphold the demilitarization of the Federal territory and to use all the means in its power to prevent the formation of new combat forces of any kind whatsoever'. Shortly after, in December, the Allies followed this up with a law to eliminate militarism: life imprisonment was to be the penalty for the very activities which were already being considered as a possibility.

Only a few months later the Allies began to urge the establishment of a German military liaison office. Adenauer was not disinclined. As early as May 1950 he set up an office 'to advise the Federal Chancellor on Security Matters' in the Federal Chancellor's Office. For the time being the new office remained a secret. It was headed by General Gerhard Count Schwerin, a much decorated soldier who had proved his worth in the Resistance. After their first encounter Adenauer declared with amazement that he did not seem at all like a general, but like a perfectly reasonable human being.

After the outbreak of the Korean War in June 1950 the question of German military co-operation became even more urgent. But Adenauer was worried about how the public would react, and he could not make up his mind to come into the open. So, unknown to the public, the office was extended and more officials were hired, until the inevitable happened: in October the press got hold of the story.

What disturbed public opinion most was the secrecy of the affair. What was to be done? Adenauer decided to make Schwerin carry the can. He declared that the General had exceeded his brief and had handed in his resignation, having been strongly urged to do so. Arnulf Baring describes this episode in detail: he says Adenauer refused to see Schwerin and surreptitiously spread the rumour that Schwerin had already begun to negotiate with industry and place contracts, which was nonsense, of course.

Schwerin was succeeded by the trade unionist Theodor Blank, who was not encumbered with either a military past or a title. Blank further enlarged and developed the so-called Blank Office, so that after the Paris Treaties had been ratified in the summer of 1955 it was able to become an ordinary Ministry of Defence.

Before that however there were many dramatic confrontations. The SPD believed that under no circumstances should the two Germanies be involved in mutually hostile military alliances. They invented the highly effective slogan *Ohne Mich* ('Without me'), and launched a campaign which was supported with complete conviction by wide sections of the public. Many officers were disillusioned by the way they had been defamed by the Allies and misled and misused by Hitler, and they never wanted to 'serve' again. Some were of the considered opinion that Germany should never again have an army. Finally the Opposition made two objections: first that the far-reaching decision to rearm had been taken simply on the authority of the Federal Government without consulting the Assembly; and secondly that the emergent Ministry of Defence was being quietly financed from the Government's housekeeping fund.

For years the Germans depended on the Occupying Powers, not only before but also after the foundation of the Federal Republic. The government did not even have a police force. No minister, not even the Federal Chancellor could give an order to the police guard standing outside his office. After the experience of two world wars it seemed that the Allies at first felt that the weaker the Germans were, the safer they themselves would be.

With the outbreak of the Korean War in June 1950 first the Americans and then the British realized that a strong West Germany was in their best interest. The French had not progressed so far: at the time they were busy annexing the Saar, previously an occupation zone, and a rich coal-mining area which they had always aspired to possess. For a long time Adenauer had resisted the French plans for the Saar, but in vain. Then in May 1950, just as all efforts were about to be abandoned, the French Foreign Secretary Robert Schumann suggested the formation of a West European Coal and Steel Community, thereby divesting the Saar question of its national aspect. Konrad Adenauer agreed enthusiastically, because this plan exactly coincided with his own idea of a new continental order in Western Europe. In 1952 the Schumann Plan united the six West European States in the Coal and Steel Community.

A few months later, in September 1950, a conference of Foreign Ministers was held in New York. This represented an important step forward in many respects. It was here that the change in the basic attitude of the Occupying Powers towards the Federal Republic first became completely clear.

Until now conferences of this type had always tried to hinder the natural progress of political development, but in New York the participants were trying to find a formula that would be valid for the future.

For West Germany this was an important station on the road which led from taking orders to making agreements. Moreover, most of her economic restrictions were lifted at this conference, and her foreign policy was given a wider scope. From September 1950 onwards foreign missions were accredited to the Federal government and no longer to the High Commission; and the consulates-general in London, Paris, and Washington were given diplomatic status.

The New York Conference was also significant for the security of the Federal Republic. Until then the debate about European defence had started from the premise that the Rhine might need defending, but never the Elbe. It was decided that henceforth every attack on the Federal Republic, including Berlin, would rate as an attack on the Occupying Powers. This meant that in the event of such an attack all the partners in the Atlantic Treaty would automatically be obliged to come to the aid of the Federal Republic. And, finally, it was decided that the Allies were no longer at war with Germany.

There is, incidentally, a passage in the Foreign Ministers' declaration which helps to explain why Bonn went on clinging to the fiction that the Federal government could speak for the whole of Germany – something which seems hard to understand today. The text says, 'Until the unification of Germany the three governments regard the government of the Federal Republic as the only freely and legitimately constituted German government: it alone, therefore, has the right to speak for the German people in the name of Germany at international conferences.' This meant that *de jure* the Federal government was regarded as the legal successor to the government of the Reich. It was an interesting change in the Allies' viewpoint; since until then they had based their refusal to use the Hague Convention on the argument that with capitulation the German state had ceased to exist.

Although on paper this represented a complete reversal of the Occupying Powers' former practice, yet the Federal government was forced to go on struggling every step of the way. Adenauer was a master at this. His basic principle was simply that gaining trust was more important than anything else. But within this framework he was quick as lightning to use every opportunity that arose. He made no demands likely to cause suspicion among the Occupying Powers, but he clung to his rights with grim tenacity and was clever at making the most of any impatience shown by the Opposition or the people as a whole. He did this chiefly by means of cunningly placed interviews, preferably in the American press.

These qualities proved particularly successful in the years between 1952 and 1955, when he led the exceedingly complicated negotiations about the German Peace Treaty and rearmament, and had to put up with innumerable disappointments and set-backs. The Peace Treaty, also known as the General Treaty (*Deutschlandvertrag*), between America, France, and Great Britain on the one hand and the Federal Republic on the other was to replace the Occupation Statute of May 1949. In other words, it was to give the Federal Republic full powers over its internal and external affairs, and to make it an equal partner in protecting European security.

The Treaty established the relations between Bonn and the Occupying Powers as well as the rights of the Allied forces who were to remain on German soil. Article Five gave certain emergency powers to the Occupying Powers in case of an attack on the Federal Republic or of an internal upheaval with which the Bonn government was unable to deal on its own. These emergency powers were only abolished in 1968 with the emergency laws promulgated by the Federal Assembly.

The General Treaty was linked with the European Defence Community Treaty (EDC) which was to ensure German rearmament and at the same time calm French fears on this subject. The Treaty members were: the Federal Republic, France, Italy, and the Benelux countries. Adenauer had always been determined to bring Germany into NATO. But he could see that because of the French an interim position (the EDC) was necessary. 'There is no doubt in my mind that if we join the European Defence Community, we shall one day quite naturally become members of the Atlantic Pact as well', he said in the Federal Assembly on 7 February 1952.

Negotiations for the two linked Treaties had been concluded by the middle of May: the General Treaty was to be signed in Bonn on 23 May, and the EDC Treaty in Paris on the 27th. The three Foreign Secretaries including Robert Schumann arrived in Bonn – in itself an extraordinary event at that time. Suddenly the French cabinet decided to make further conditions before signing. It seemed as though years of negotiation had been in vain. 'All my efforts to diminish mistrust of Germany seem to have had little success' a saddened and disappointed Adenauer wrote in his memoirs.[16] His cool, dry account of what happened gives no idea of the confusion caused by France's sudden change of mind. Amazingly, after three days of discussion they succeeded in agreeing on fresh modifications and formulations. At last, as Adenauer writes: 'On 26 May at 10 am the German Treaty was solemnly signed in the big hall of the Federal Assembly.' No representative of the SPD was present at the ceremony. Adenauer bitterly notes that the Opposition leader Schumacher called the act of signature 'the crude celebration of their victory over the German people by a coalition of the Allies with the clergy', and that he launched the slogan, 'whoever agrees with the General Treaty ceases to be a good German'.

It had originally been Adenauer's wish to celebrate the occasion in a particularly festive way: he wanted it to make a profound impression on the people. Arnulf Baring writes:

> Long before 26 May Adenauer had been looking forward to the day of signing, and had made all the preparations for a joyous

celebration. As Paul Weymar reports, the protocol file contains several notes about this in Adenauer's own hand. ... Otto Lenz had persuaded the Chancellor to have a torchlight procession, and the Federal Minister for Home Affairs asked all the *Land* governments to fly flags on public buildings, to give the children a holiday, and to make sure they understood the meaning of the Treaty.

But nothing came of all that. The Social Democrats as well as the *Land* governments ruined the Chancellor's plan. The *Länder* – some through the appropriate ministry and some by cabinet decision – refused to comply with the Chancellor's wishes: not even their governments, let alone the school teachers, they said, had been properly informed of the content of the Treaties.

On 23 May the parliamentary SPD had forced a sitting of the Assembly: they had not succeeded in obtaining a last-minute debate on the Treaties, but at least they had spoiled the Chancellor's pleasure. For of course it upset him to hear representative Adolf Arndt publicly asking the Coalition parties whether in the course of the coming celebrations they were prepared to rejoice over something they had not seen and which they had refused to discuss in public.

Arndt found support even among representatives belonging to the Coalition parties, especially when he objected to the torch-light procession: in the recent past, he said, a torchlight procession had set the whole of Germany on fire. In any case, there was so much reluctance even in the ranks of Adenauer's own party, that the torchlight procession was dropped. ... On 25 May the Federal Chancellor publicly requested that the Treaty should not be celebrated except at the actual ceremony of signing. The Germans needed to become completely familiar with the contents of the Treaty before they could appreciate the progress made.'[17]

There is something uncommonly tragic about this episode. One feels sorry for the seventy-eight-year-old Chancellor: how often he must have asked himself whether he would live to complete the work for which he had fought so stubbornly and steadily against such heavy opposition. No one felt like celebrating. For many this was the moment for relinquishing all hope of ever reunifying Germany – a hope which in those days seemed far from Utopian. Even Adenauer had constantly cherished it, or at any rate paid it constant lip-service. The utter loneliness of this old man becomes apparent with his acceptance of the idea of a torchlight procession, an idea as un-Adenauerish as can possibly be imagined. He wanted to do something out of the ordinary – right outside his normal, bleak, austere everyday world.

As though to justify himself, in his memoirs Adenauer expounds his philosophy and his reasons for orienting the Federal Republic so exclusively towards the West: 'Wishing alone can't make a policy, especially if you are weak. Only when the West has grown strong will there be a true basis for peace talks with the aim of liberating not only the Soviet Union, but the whole of Eastern Europe from its slavery behind the Iron Curtain – and of liberating them without going to war.[18]'

It is strange to read these sentences written in 1953. 'Only when the West has grown strong . . .'; it is exactly what the CDU/CSU are still saying today, thirty years later. And in the year 2000 they will still be thinking that when the West has grown really strong and is growing even stronger, then the day will come when the Russians run out of steam and say to themselves, there is no point in going on; we ought to give in.

Neither Adenauer himself nor his successors seem to have realized that it was then, at the beginning of the fifties, that the West reached its maximum strength: the Russians had only just tested their first atom bomb. And now, although we are spending unconscionable sums on armaments, we are not as strong as we were then, and probably never will be again. The only difference made by these colossal efforts is that today all the nations together are spending about $500 billion on armaments, whereas thirty years ago it was $50 billion.

Adenauer's assessment of the Treaty was as follows:

The Treaty with the three Powers restored her freedom of action to the Federal Republic. It entitled her, under international law, to sign the European Defence Pact. She was able once again to sign treaties and engage in alliances. ... The foundation of the European Defence Community gave the Federal Republic a firm link with the Atlantic Pact. In joining the European Defence Community the Federal government was able to realize one of its aims, namely Germany's entry into a European Community which, in its turn, was linked to a worldwide network of treaties set up by the free world in order to preserve peace. No longer did we stand alone. No longer were we merely the object of other nations' foreign policy. A great historical change took place in that May of 1952: its impact must have struck anyone who remembered the May of 1945, when the full extent of the German catastrophe became apparent. In 1949 we signed the constitution of the Federal Republic in the hall of the Federal Council; three years later, on 26 May 1952, our right of independent action under international law was restored to us in that very same hall.[19]

So now the Peace Treaty was signed – despite agitated protests not only by the Opposition, but also by members of the CDU, especially by Brentano, and the ministers Dehler, Blücher, and Jakob Kaiser. Their main objection was the so-called binding clause which said that in the case of German reunification the Federal Republic would still be bound by the Treaty. It was signed, but it was far from home and dry. True, the American Senate and the British parliament ratified it before the end of the year, and the Federal Assembly followed shortly after with 226 votes in favour and 164 against, but 1952 and 1953 went by without the French Assembly declaring their position. And during the first six months of 1954 nothing stirred in Paris either. The number of Frenchmen opposed to the EDC was obviously still growing. They objected to the supra-national character of the EDC, and with the help of other member states they tried to make further changes. In fact, on 30 August 1954 the French National Assembly decided by 319 votes in favour and 264 against to remove the ratification of the treaty from the agenda: they had kept their partners waiting more than two years. That was the end of the EDC.

The Chancellor wrote in his memoirs: 'For Germany, the result of the vote in the French National Assembly destroyed the fruit of all her prolonged efforts to regain her sovereignty; and of all her efforts to take a step forward towards the reconstruction of Europe. All those efforts – all those struggles! And who has emerged victorious? No doubt about it; it is Moscow; and she owes her victory to the 100 Communist votes (more or less) which carried the day in the French National Assembly.

These terrible days are deeply engraved on my memory, but sorrow and resignation do no good. The tasks of getting Germany accepted among the free nations and of creating Europe had to be tackled once more.'[20]

The shot in the air from Paris was quickly followed by a ray of light from London. A British–American working-party led by Anthony Eden had an idea of genius: the Brussels Pact signed in 1948 by Great Britain, France, and Benelux as a protection *against* Germany could be altered and given a new purpose by including Germany in the alliance. This shows what can be done in politics if the desire to find a solution is strong enough.

The Brussels Pact was an extension of a treaty of alliance originally signed by France and Great Britain at Dunkirk in 1947 to ward off any possible 'German aggression'. Now Eden suggested that the Federal Republic and Italy should also be included in a pact that postulated that in the event of an attack on one of its members the others should automatically be bound to come to its aid. The pact would thus become a substitute for the EDC.

The Treaty, now called the Treaty of Paris, was signed in Paris in October 1954 and came into effect in May 1955. It marked the end of the Occupation regime and gave Germany back the sovereignty she had lost nine years before. At the same time it was decided that Germany should make a contribution to the defence system stipulated by the various treaties between Western Europe and the USA.

The obligation to rearm was immediately implemented.

On 12 November 1955 the first 101 officers led by General Heusinger and General Speidel were sworn in by Theodor Blank in the carriage hall of the Ermekeil barracks. Only ten of the 101 were in uniform – the tailors had not been able to finish their work in time. This ceremony marked the birth of the *Bundeswehr*. Five years later, in 1960, it numbered 300,000 men, and 30 billion marks had been spent on setting it up.

The Paris Treaty was the most important Germany has ever signed, and that is why I have described every phase of the work that went into it. It ended with Germany regaining her sovereignty and joining the West European Union and the Atlantic Pact. One more episode that took place during that period should be recounted: the story of the Russian note.

On 10 March 1952 the Soviets handed the three Allied Powers a note whose significance was to be discussed amongst Germans for the next ten years. It read:

> It is understood that a peace treaty will have to be drafted with the direct participation of Germany represented by a government of the *whole country*. It follows, therefore, that the USSR, the USA, Great Britain and France who exercise a controlling function in Germany must discover what conditions would be favourable for urgently expediting the formation of a government of the whole of Germany that would express the will of the German people.... The need to hasten the conclusion of a peace treaty with Germany is dictated by the danger of a recrudescence of German militarism which has already unleashed two world wars; the danger is still present, because the relevant decisions of the Potsdam Conference have not yet been implemented.

The 'political guidelines' set out in the note were as follows: the restoration of German unity; the departure of all the Occupying Powers; all the basic rights of democracy to be guaranteed, including freedom of the press, freedom of political thought, and freedom of assembly; the abolition of all economic restrictions; a national fighting force adequate to defend the country; and, finally, Germany must undertake not to enter into any coalition or military pact aimed at any country whose forces had participated in the war against her.

Adenauer's reaction was as follows: 'Evidently the Soviet Union felt the moment had come to make another attempt to hinder the development of European unity and, if possible, to destroy it. For, mark you, the negotiations over the European Defence Community and the General Treaty had almost been concluded. Obviously the Soviet Union was trying to prevent the integration of the Federal Republic into the West. And in fact the best way of doing this was by neutralizing Germany as the Soviet Union planned to do. Without Germany the integration of Europe was bound to fail from the very beginning.'[21]

The Social Democrats thereupon rejected the treaties signed in May 1952, because they thought that the note of 10 May might after all present possibilities for a peaceful unification of Germany, which would first have to be examined. The SPD particularly objected to rearming the Federal Republic on the grounds that the constitution had made no provision for a fighting force: the constitution would therefore have to be amended. Eventually 144 representatives, including all the SPD members, lodged a complaint with the Federal constitutional court. But the court decided that the appeal to uphold the incompatibility of a German military contribution with the constitution was not admissible at that moment, because the legislative bodies had not yet concluded their deliberations. In other words, the ratification of the Treaty was not prevented, and so history passed over this episode as over many another.

1955 was an eventful year. February saw the fall in the USSR of Malenkov who had introduced the first *détente*; Khrushchev now assumed the leadership in Moscow. In March, after 157 negotiating sessions, the Russians suddenly signed the Austrian Peace Treaty; following that the Kremlin chiefs journeyed to Belgrade to mark their reconciliation with Tito. After all these preparations the summer of 1955 saw the first major appearance by the Soviet leadership on the Western stage. The First Secretary of the Soviet Communist Party, Khrushchev, and Prime Minister Bulganin, came to a summit conference at Geneva. These two gentlemen radiated joviality; they brought with them General Shukov, the conqueror of Berlin – presumably to remind General Eisenhower of their brotherhood-in-arms during the Second World War. It was the first meeting between the Western heads of state and the Soviet government chiefs since the Potsdam conference in July 1945.

The most interesting suggestion at the Geneva conference (which otherwise ended without a single new idea) came from Anthony Eden. It was that a reunited Germany should join the four Powers meeting at Geneva, America, Great Britain, France, and the Soviet Union, in a Five-Power Pact: each would be obliged to come to the aid of the others in case of an attack. It was an interesting suggestion, but unrealistic of course, because the Soviets kept repeating everything they had said before and added a new demand, which was that if Germany were reunited, the GDR should be allowed to keep its 'achievements'. The only advantage for the FRG that came out of the conference was the declaration that the European security system desired by the Russians would have to be linked to the reunification of Germany. The 'directive' intended for the conference of Foreign Ministers which was to take place in the autumn (also in Geneva) included the following passage: 'The Heads of State recognize their joint responsibility for the solution of the German question and the reunification of Germany; they have agreed that these must be pursued by means of free elections in harmony with the national interest of the German people and also of the interests of European security.'

This was the last time the Soviets agreed to such a clause. The truth is that all hope of German reunification finally vanished with this summit conference: the Russian leaders were merely pretending to be co-operative. The subsequent conference of Foreign Ministers in the autumn of 1955 incontrovertibly showed that only the permanent partition of Germany was acceptable to the Russians. 'The spirit of Geneva' that characterized the short period of *détente* soon disappeared.

In June the Soviet government had already invited Adenauer to Moscow to 'discuss the question of establishing diplomatic, commercial, and cultural relations'. The Federal government replied that the 'question of Germany's national unity and the liberation of those Germans who are still detained on Soviet territory' would also have to be on the agenda; in other words, the question of reunification and of the prisoners of war. The Russians agreed, and Adenauer set out in the autumn of 1955.

It was a very strange journey, especially for anyone who remembered that sixteen years previously, in the autumn of 1939, a German Foreign Secretary by the name of Joachim von Ribbentrop had also landed at Moscow airport. At that time the swastika flag had fluttered peacefully beside the flag with the hammer and sickle. Ribbentrop had come to seal the pact between the two arch-tyrants, Hitler and Stalin. A stay of twenty-four hours was enough to divide up the world from the Baltic to the Black Sea between the two dictators.

Since that autumn of 1939 there had been no official German visit to Moscow, so it may be imagined that the Soviet leaders also looked forward to this meeting with curiosity. In September 1955 Adenauer and his delegation arrived with much pomp and circumstance in two special planes and a special train. Wilhelm Grewe, at that time head of the political section of the Foreign Office, explains the reason for the special train: 'The special train stationed in a siding of the Moscow railway station had special bug-proof carriages, a Mitropa dining-car, radio and telephone equipment, office compartments, and so on – in other words it was a peripatetic embassy whose installation we had demanded in the preliminary procedural talks to compensate for the absence of a real embassy.'[22]

The Chancellor was received with much ceremony: Prime

Minister Bulganin, Foreign Secretary Molotov, Deputy Foreign Ministers Gromyko and Semyonov, as well as the chief ideologue Suslov, were all lined up in a row. The same national anthems were played as they had been sixteen years before; the flags fluttered in the wind, but only one was still the same. The guard of honour was specially chosen and made up of very young, splendid-looking lads who were wearing the colourful parade uniform for the first time it had been worn since 1917. They produced the intended effect of determination, concentration, precision on all of us. In the evening there was a great gala banquet with high-sounding toasts, expansive hospitality, and general fraternization. The next day the two declarations of intent were read out. The German declaration was a masterpiece of restrained remorse and spontaneous warmth combined with a call for a new beginning. The next day the practical talks began, and a deep rift immediately became apparent.

The diplomatic relations desired by the Soviet Union posed an exceedingly tricky problem for the Federal government. If both the GDR and the FRG were to maintain ambassadors in Russia that might lead to a change of policy on the part of those nations who considered the Federal Republic as the only legitimate representative of the German people and therefore had no diplomatic relations with the GDR. On the other hand, it was for this very reason that the Soviets were very keen to resume diplomatic relations: two German ambassadors in Moscow would be visible proof that there were two States. So the German Federal Chancellor could hope to get something very special in return for such a concession. In his memoirs he says that for him the most important issue was the prisoners of war.

But according to the Soviets, there were no prisoners of war in the Soviet Union, 'only war criminals from the Hitler armies; in other words, 9,628 rapists, arsonists, and murderers'. Anyone who accompanied Adenauer to Moscow knows quite well that his first priority was a concession regarding

the reunification of Germany at any rate until this was cate-
gorically refused by the Russians.

Charles Bohlen, the then US Ambassador to Moscow,
thinks Adenauer allowed himself to be led into a trap; it was
a trap because in the end he was forced to accept a far from
satisfactory agreement. Bohlen thought that it was a mistake
for a Head of State to go to Moscow in order to do business
there with full diplomatic recognition.[23]

Up to a point the German diplomat Wilhelm Grewe shares
that view: 'If Adenauer made a false calculation in his visit to
Moscow, it was this: he thought his visit could be a mere
starting-point for other negotiations which would not have
to be carried on under pressure of time, in the glaring light of
world publicity and could be handled by experts, or at least
by lower placed officials and not by himself . . . Adenauer had
got himself into a tight corner: he was forced to agree to a
settlement and to accept the minimum conditions which he
had previously thought of as a last resort.'[24]

Today the episode is interesting as a heuristic principle: it
should be a lesson to the CDU/CSU who never stop picking
holes in the Eastern Treaties. The disappointing experience
of the first Federal Chancellor shows that no one returns
from Moscow without having sacrificed some part of his
original intentions.

Today, moreover, we can see that there never was a chance
of reunification. But in those days things looked different.
Konrad Adenauer tells us in his memoirs how in that August
of 1955 he received a message from US Foreign Secretary
Dulles saying, 'He had the distinct impression, based on
many separate observations, that the Soviet attitude had soft-
ened. He was more than ever convinced that reunification
would come, even though perhaps a few years – he meant two
to four – might pass before it did. If the Soviets were not yet
ready to make concessions, that was solely because they felt
they had to take the mood of the satellite countries into
account. The governments of these countries would feel en-

dangered if Moscow were to drop the 'Pankow-Regime' (East Berlin) at this moment.'[25]

But a month later in Moscow Khrushchev told Adenauer that the Federal Republic had had plenty of warning before signing the Paris Treaties and before joining NATO, but Bonn had refused to listen. And now, he said, 'the reunification of Germany has come to mean that a *united* Germany would belong to NATO – and this when NATO was created purely in opposition to the Soviet Union. The truth of this is proved by everything that has occurred. It is also proved by the fact that our wish to join NATO was refused. It was refused because NATO has been created in opposition to the Soviet Union and the other People's Democracies! But if an organization is set up against us, then we, as statesmen, will do everything we can to weaken that organization.'

The meetings were frequently turbulent. Khrushchev boasted, 'The wind is not blowing in *our* face.' Adenauer too gave vent to his anger, 'Foreign Secretary Molotov said the Germans were incapable of throwing off Hitler's yoke. Permit me to ask a question: who was it who signed an agreement with Hitler: you or I?' Adenauer says in his memoirs: 'Khrushchev became very agitated, and not everything could be translated, because he spoke too fast. From time to time he made threatening gestures with his fists. So then I got up and shook my fists back at him.'[26]

But the Federal Chancellor also describes episodes which show a friendly, relaxed, almost affectionate atmosphere: 'The weather was splendid and we sat on the terrace of the dacha and talked very freely with one another...' In a conversation alone with him, Khrushchev returned to the subject of Red China. He described it as the greatest problem:

'Imagine, there are already more than 600 million people in Red China. Every year there are 12 million more. And all of them people who can live on a handful of rice. Whatever – and here he clasped his hands – whatever is to come of it?'

I thought [Adenauer continues]: My friend, one day you'll be quite glad that you don't have to go on maintaining troops in the

West!... Suddenly Khrushchev said out of the blue: 'It is a problem we can solve. But it is very hard. And that is why I am asking you: help us to deal with Red China!' And after some hesitation he added: 'And with the Americans ...'

Khrushchev begged me to help him three times during my visit to Moscow. I never responded. It would have been disloyal to Europe and America; and to help the Russians at that stage and without any firm ties with the rest of the free world would have been putting one's head in the lion's jaws. I had no doubt about that.[27]

After further dramatic and totally fruitless sessions the Chancellor finally gave up; he ordered the planes for the return journey a day sooner than planned. Realizing this, the Russians made a U-turn that very day. During the gala dinner Bulganin privately told Adenauer that if the Federal Republic would declare its intention of resuming diplomatic relations, the Soviet leaders would give their word of honour that the prisoners of war should start on their journey home within a week. And that is what happened, though naturally only after much argument within the German delegation. 'After all that had happened, Brentano and Hallstein were particularly opposed to resuming diplomatic relations: how could I agree when no progress at all had been made on the reunification question?', Adenauer writes in his memoirs.[28]

On the flight home the delegation anxiously discussed how they were going to break it to the German people that they had agreed to exchange ambassadors without obtaining any concessions on the question of reunification. 'We shall cop it', was the general feeling. How great was their amazement when they were received with tremendous rejoicing at the Cologne-Wahn airport: everyone was talking about the prisoners of war coming home – reunification was not even mentioned. For the next few days the whole press – (with the exception of *Die Zeit*) – took the same line.

Up to this point public opinion in Germany had been totally directed towards ending the partition of the country. But from the very beginning, there were two theories on how to bring this about. The Conservatives were for a policy of strength – rearmament and threats – while the Social Democrats wanted not to rearm and not to join NATO, but to do everything possible to relax tension and return to normal conditions. The resumption of diplomatic relations in 1955 might have been a first step towards normal conditions. But it turned out otherwise. During the next few years all contact was avoided, and ten years went by before another official visitor from Bonn arrived in Moscow, the then Secretary of State and present Federal President Karl Carstens.

However, as both sides continued to rearm the cry for reunification became a mere ritual, and fewer and fewer people believed in it. But the old disagreement between the Conservatives and the Opposition remained.

In a modified form this disagreement persists today and determines political argument in the Federal Republic. Basically the 1980 elections to the Bundestag were dominated by two alternatives: the CDU/CSU accused Chancellor Schmidt of betraying his Allies because, in spite of Afghanistan, he went to talk to Brezhnev in Moscow. They complained that there was a 'Moscow group' in the SPD. The SPD and the FDP retorted by saying that the policy of strength as advocated by the CDU/CSU was a danger to peace. So whether or not to have *détente* was the watchword for 1980, as it had been in the past.

The pseudo-theological battle between the preachers of the strength doctrine and the faithful of the *détente* gospel tends to turn this political question into a moral category: it is no longer a question of alternatives and compromises, but of the pure, unadulterated truth. As a result, the obvious solution to a problem has often been overlooked: no one has applied a sensible mixture of strength and willingness to compromise in proportions appropriate to a given situation. Adenauer's policy was obviously based on the somewhat unrealistic idea that the Russians would 'capitulate'; Brandt and Schmidt were wrong in expecting their policy of *détente* to yield constant and far too rapid results.

And by an irony of fate it always turns out that when

developments seem to corroborate one view rather than the other, and public opinion is just about to swing in its favour, something or other happens to tip the whole situation over in the other direction. That is what occurred in 1955 and 1956: first the 'spirit of Geneva' had a slightly emollient influence on the inflexibility of the Conservatives; then the events of Suez and Hungary turned the tide the other way.

Détente shyly re-emerged in 1959, but then the Cuba crisis crushed it. Before Cuba there was a phase when people in the Federal Republic began to think that an understanding with the East would have to be bought at the expense of the recognition of 'realities' – like the existence of a second German State. Then came the crisis and Kennedy's reaction, which forced Khrushchev to transport his stockpile of rockets from Cuba back to the USSR: and the same people who had been prepared to recognize 'realities' said, Thank God we didn't make any sacrifices; obviously it would have been quite unnecessary.

And yet, after the progress made in the early seventies, hope was once more succeeded by disappointment when the Russian divisions marched into Afghanistan at the end of the decade. The Federal government adopted the slogan '*détente is divisible*' and hoped that it would help to keep at least Central Europe out of the intensifying freeze-up between Washington and Moscow; but the events of 1981 in Poland again produced an instinctive reaction: the desire for total segregation.

By 1953 Adenauer had become pretty invulnerable on the home front. The economy was booming and the CDU/CSU were only one seat short of absolute majority: this was because the 1953 elections had been dominated by the impact of 17 June, when a rising of East Berlin workers was put down by Russian tanks. Four years later, in 1957, the party easily won a complete majority, but in order to give his government as broad a base as possible, the Chancellor had formed a coalition with the liberals (FDP) and smaller parties.

Ever since Thomas Dehler had become Chairman of the FDP, friction had grown in the coalition. Dehler was a strong independent personality, an emotional firebrand, a charismatic speaker always inclined to rebel, and he was far more interested in reunification than in integration with the West. He had often given the Chancellor trouble in the past. It was he who had pointed out that the real decisions in Bonn bypassed the cabinet and the Assembly because Adenauer monopolized the High Commissioners. Dehler was always inveighing against the Paris Treaties and particularly angered Adenauer when, after the failure of the European Defence Community, he declared, 'The Catholic statesmen have failed in their attempt to integrate Europe, and it must not be repeated'. Adenauer thought the reference to the Catholic threesome, Adenauer, de Gaspery and Robert Schumann, was a perfidious attempt to revive North German Protestant animosity. But Dehler did not fail to hit his true target: the Federal Chancellor's heart.

The FDP was much given to rhetorical escapades of this sort, especially after it became clear in the autumn of 1955 that the Soviet Union was determined to keep Germany divided for ever. For in Moscow on 20 September 1955, right after Adenauer had left, the Soviet Union signed a treaty with the GDR in which the Russians recognized the 'full sovereignty' of East Germany. The Control Commission was to have no more right of decision-making, and the Soviet High Commission was to be wound up. But the Soviet troops would remain! The three Western Powers regarded this as a breach of the Allied agreement regarding Germany, and lodged a sharp protest: 'The three governments are of the opinion that the Soviet Union remains bound to her obligations towards the Three Powers in regard to Germany. In particular they hold that the undertakings exchanged on 20 September 1955 between Deputy Foreign Secretary Sorin and Foreign Secretary Bolz do not relieve the Soviet Union of her obligations regarding transport and communications between the various parts of Germany, including Berlin.'

It soon became obvious how necessary this protest was. On 29 November there was an incident in Berlin which the Americans took very seriously. For the first time since the Four Powers occupied the city an American military vehicle was stopped by officers of the People's Police. Among the passengers were two American Congress members. The Americans immediately protested to the Soviet Town Commandant; but he refused to accept the protest and declared that the vehicle had been stopped in accordance with the laws of the German Democratic Republic. Thereupon the American ambassador James Conant sent a protest to Pushkin, the Soviet Ambassador in East Berlin: 'You will understand that the government of the United States will continue to hold the Soviet authorities responsible for the safety of all American citizens and for their treatment so long as they are in areas under Soviet authority and control, including the Soviet sector of Berlin.'

Konrad Adenauer pondered what could have caused this sudden deterioration and the negation of 'the spirit of Geneva'. In his memoirs he reports a conversation between the then envoy and later ambassador, von Welck, and an important American official. 'Welck reports,' wrote the Chancellor, 'that the Americans think "the spirit of Geneva" may be causing the Soviet government quite a headache. Everywhere in the satellite states, in the Russian occupied Zone, and even in the Soviet Union people are beginning to sniff the morning air: everyone is expecting a relaxation of the regime. This emanation from "the spirit of Geneva" could be so dangerous for the Soviet government that they might even prefer to start the Cold War again.'[29]

Strangely enough though, Adenauer did not conclude from this report that since *détente* was so effective, it would be better to cultivate it than to stake everything on rearmament: on the contrary, he went on insisting that no change could be expected in the Soviet attitude until Russia realized that she would have to abandon her aim of neutralizing Germany and dominating the whole of Western Europe. Therefore he energetically opposed every initiative put up by the FDP to solve the unification question. Such initiatives 'only awaken false hopes and do damage', the Chancellor said.

1956 was the year of the famous double crisis: the Anglo-French attack on Suez on 31 October, and the brutal suppression of the Hungarian rising by the Russians in the first days of November. It so happened that it was on the very day of the Suez crisis that Adenauer made his first trip to Paris. The description in his memoirs, usually such a detailed account, is strangely perfunctory, perhaps because the background to the Suez affair remains mysterious to this day.

In a written report to Adenauer dated 31 October 1956, Foreign Secretary von Brentano writes: 'Most of the gentlemen I spoke to quite openly alluded to the fact that England and France had evidently encouraged Israel to invade in order to have an excuse for intervening.' Why exactly they wanted to intervene remains obscure. In my opinion, they showed the belated reflexes of colonial powers who have not quite got used to seeing their former dominions ruled by independent and inconvenient masters; in other words, they wanted to get rid of Nasser.

The conflict was triggered off in July when President Nasser nationalized the General Suez Canal Company. He needed its revenues to build the Aswan Dam. England and France had originally agreed to finance this, but had withdrawn their offer. On 29 October Israeli troops crossed the Egyptian frontier on the Sinai peninsula and began marching towards the Suez Canal. The next day London and Paris sent an ultimatum to Israel and Egypt demanding that ten kilometres on either side of the Canal be cleared of troops. The next day French and British air forces bombed the Canal Zone in preparation to landing a Franco-British expeditionary force. When British paratroops were dropped, the commandant of Port Said started negotiations to capitulate.

At this point Moscow threatened to intervene with her full striking power unless peace were re-established immediately. Washington also began to threaten. For the first time ever the

USA and the USSR voted together in the UN against two NATO members. Finally in the night of 6–7 November everyone concerned agreed to the UN's demand for a cease-fire.

At exactly the same moment the Soviet Union decided to put a bloody end to the rising in Hungary which had begun in October with students demonstrating in favour of democratic freedom. The Russians acted with great brutality. During the rising, Prime Minister Imre Nagy, who had been deposed the year before, returned to head the government, and the rising turned into a full-scale revolution. Nagy announced the withdrawal of Hungary from the Warsaw Pact and declared her neutrality. On 4 November the Russians finally crushed the rising in spite of grim resistance.

Soon after I had the opportunity to discuss the tragedy of this double crisis with Nehru, and he told me that at the time the Russian Ambassador had told him that the Kremlin thought the Suez escapade would be the beginning of a Third World War: they could not imagine that France and Britain would launch such an important military action without the knowledge of the United States. It was because of this, Nehru thought, that the reaction in Hungary had been so violent: Moscow was determined not to lose any part of her sphere of influence at that moment. It sounded very plausible at the time. But after the events of Prague and Afghanistan we can be pretty sure that the Soviet reaction in Hungary would not have been much different anyway.

Wilhelm Grewe, who accompanied the Chancellor on his first visit to Paris, describes a conversation between Adenauer and the then Prime Minister Guy Mollet: 'In the course of his argument Adenauer allowed himself to be carried away to criticize the American leadership and its policies so strongly that Foreign Secretary Heinrich von Brentano felt impelled – and was not ashamed – to show that he did not share these views. For two and a half years, Adenauer insisted, letters had passed between the White House and the Kremlin without the participation of the State Department. When challenged, Dulles had not denied this correspondence. The idea behind it seemed to be that world peace needed to be guaranteed by a balance between the two atomic Powers. There might even be a notion that the two Superpowers should divide up the world and act as its umpires. Adenauer disliked the ambiguity implicit in this American policy which disregarded the interests of the other Allies, diminished the importance of Europe, and meant the US abandoning her leading role in NATO.'

Grewe adds: 'Adenauer's attitude to America as a whole and to the leading personalities there was much the same as towards his colleagues, his friends in the party, and to many others in his circle. His relations with most of those whom he had to see regularly were subject to violent fluctuations and were constantly overshadowed by attacks of suspicion such as I have described. Adenauer imagined that during the period of his Presidency, Eisenhower was carrying on a foreign policy all of his own which he had hatched in secret correspondence with the Kremlin: this was a figment of Adenauer's suspicion without any basis in the events of 1956.'[30]

It was only towards France that Adenauer suppressed his mistrust, especially towards Charles de Gaulle, who actually deserved it more than anyone else. For Adenauer, reconciliation with France was the most important problem and goal of German foreign policy. His strong emphasis on France led to a reaction inside his own party: a group emerged whose members felt that Adenauer was neglecting Britain and America, whereas they believed that in the twentieth century the USA was really far more important. In order to define this disagreement people spoke of a French and an Anglo-American party within the CDU/CSU. While Adenauer headed the so-called French party, Ludwig Erhard was said to be the leader of the Anglo-American party.

From spring to autumn 1957 the German people were kept in a state of breathless excitement by passionate disputes over nuclear weapons. The question was whether the *Bundeswehr*, the new armed forces, should have atomic weapons. Even the stockpiling of American nuclear weapons in the Federal Republic caused violent discussions. Adenauer made his point of view clear in a press conference. The Federal Republic, he said, had opted not to produce such weapons, but he insisted that the army must be equipped with tactical atomic weapons 'which are no more than a development of ordinary artillery'; otherwise the soldiers of the Federal Republic would be less well equipped than any of their colleagues in NATO, and that would be discrimination. At this, protests rained down upon the Chancellor from all sides. Eighteen famous atomic scientists sent a telegram of protest, Albert Schweitzer issued a proclamation which had a great effect and the slogan 'Fight Atomic Death' was seen and heard everywhere.

The SPD was strictly opposed to Adenauer's views. Their leader Erich Ollenhauer declared that if his party were to win the September elections they would abolish military service, forbid the equipment of the *Bundeswehr* with atomic weapons, and see to it that the Western Allies stopped stockpiling atomic weapons in the Federal Republic. The programme was enormously popular.

Nevertheless, the CDU/CSU won the election with a total majority. Not least among the reasons for this was the fact that most people realized who had caused the failure of the disarmament conference held in London from March to September which had seemed to promise a certain degree of hope: it was the Soviet Union. This became very obvious when shortly afterwards the disarmament proposals of the West were approved in a plenary session of the UN by a big majority.

In October 1957 the Soviet Union launched its sputnik. With this spectacular military breakthrough in rocket technique it became quite clear to the world at large why Moscow was not interested in disarmament agreements. From now on the atomic race was over carriers rather than warheads.

In spite of all this 1957 ended on an optimistic note. The routine NATO conference in December was upgraded at rather short notice to a summit conference. Fifteen heads of state led by Eisenhower, as well as the Foreign and Defence ministers of the NATO countries and innumerable officials, assembled in Paris. A Frenchman who in his youth had attended the peace conference of Versailles said to me, as he gazed at this giant gathering, that it was the largest international meeting of the kind that had been seen since 1919.

The conference brought a happy surprise for those like myself who ever since the Soviet note of 1952 had regretted that none of the numerous Russian proposals had ever been discussed, if only in order to call the Russian bluff. Eisenhower spoke first, and gave an impressive performance. Adenauer was next, and everyone expected him to deliver his routine speech: 'The tension between the United States and Russia will only cease when their own experience convinces the Russians that they cannot last out the armaments race with the West, and that they must seek to come to an understanding'. But nothing of the sort happened. Having always rejected the idea of negotiating with the Russians and spoken only of the need for strength and unity, Adenauer suddenly appealed for an 'attempt to discover, by diplomatic means, what precisely are the ideas underlying the Russian proposals'. This was his reaction to a letter from Bulganin of 10 December followed by a note of 12 December. With these two missives the Russians embarked on a worldwide diplomatic offensive. They proposed a Central European zone free from atomic weapons, a non-aggression treaty between NATO and the Warsaw Pact, and an undertaking by the great Powers not to use nuclear weapons.

Everyone was astonished. Some Americans feared that Bonn was threatening to go neutral, others thought it was probably just political manœuvre by Adenauer. Both these views are refuted by Grewe, who writes that between Christmas and the New Year he worked on a reply to Bulganin which he took to the Chancellor at Rhöndorf. 'My attempt to persuade Adenauer to send an answer which could lead to real conversations with the Russians seemed to have fallen on fruitful ground.'

A little later, in the spring of 1958, Adenauer even proposed to the Russian Ambassador Smirnov that the Soviet Union should concede to the GDR the same status as Austria. This special status precluded a second *Anschluss* (union with Germany), so it would have meant renouncing the prospect of German reunification; it would also have meant a guarantee of neutrality, making integration into NATO out of the question. True, it is somewhat hard to see what could have appeared particularly enticing to Moscow about this proposal. The Soviet Union would have had to give up a good deal in exchange for nothing.

The same is true of another scheme of Adenauer's which did not see the light of day until after his death when the third volume of Adenauer Studies appeared in 1974.[31] This was the so-called Globke Plan, a sketch for a treaty whose last version dates from 1960. It is based on ideas by Konrad Adenauer, Hans Globke, and Heinrich Krone, and begins with a demand for self-determination for the people of the GDR – exactly what Moscow was determined to prevent. This document served to develop a somewhat implausible picture of Adenauer's Eastern policy. It is interesting to learn that such ideas were discussed at all. What remains unsatisfactory is that they were unrealistic and that no attempt was ever made to put them into practice.

About the same time, however, a dove of peace managed to make its way from Moscow to Bonn. In April 1958 Bulganin lost his office, which Khrushchev assumed in addition to his own. Shortly afterwards Anastas Mikoyan, the Chief Deputy Prime Minister of the Soviet Union, came to Bonn to sign treaties which had been under discussion for a long time: the trade pact, the agreement about setting up consular representations, and the agreement negotiated by Ambassador Lahr in Moscow for the return of German civilians held in the Soviet Union.

The Federal Chancellor was much taken with Mikoyan, who was lively, constantly amusing, and exceptionally intelligent. They squabbled a little over whether or not Lenin had received 20 million gold Marks from the German government, as Adenauer insisted. Mikoyan contradicted this: if it were true, he would know it, because at that time he had been very closely associated with Lenin. Adenauer had got his information from a newspaper, and in the end he wriggled out of the argument by bringing in Marx and Engels and saying that at least ideologically the USSR owed a lot to Germany. 'Yes, the Germans can be proud of that,' said Mikoyan. But in fact the historian Fritz Fisher has established that the Bolshoviks got at least 50 million Marks from Germany.[32]

By autumn 1958 the short spell of understanding was disappearing. This was heralded by Ulbricht's declaration that 'The whole of Berlin lies in the territory of the GDR. The whole of Berlin is under the sovereignty of the GDR.' Two weeks later, on 10 November, Khrushchev sounded the same note in a speech in the Moscow Stadium. On 27 November Khrushchev startled the world with a statement on Berlin addressed to the three Western Powers that has gone down in history as an 'ultimatum'. The Soviets demanded the withdrawal of all Occupation forces from Berlin within six weeks; the former capital was to become a 'demilitarized free city'. If no agreement was reached with the Western Powers within the specified period, then the Russians would hand over all their powers and functions as an Occupying Power to the GDR. The Western Powers were indignant and sharply rejected the idea of a one-sided alteration of the Four Powers' status in Berlin.

The British reply was the most impressive. Throwing tact to the winds it did not hesitate to pulverize the Russian falsification of history, according to which only the Russians and not the Western democracies had stood up to Hitler's conquests. The note reminded its recipients of the incident that preceded the Second World War: 'On August 23 the German–Soviet Non-Aggression Pact, commonly known as the Molotov-Ribbentrop Pact, was announced with such suddenness that all Europe was aghast. Her Britannic Majesty's government is astonished that the Soviet Government does not mention this pact in the historical part of its note of 27 November 1958, as the general view has always been that it was the signing of this pact that made the outbreak of war inevitable.'

The British also recalled a speech of Molotov's to the Supreme Soviet on 31 October 1939. '"The ruling circles of Great Britain and France have recently tried to present themselves as the champions of the nation's democratic rights against Hitlerism; the British government declared that in making war on Germany it intended no more and no less than to destroy Hitlerism.... But there is absolutely no justification for such a war. As with every other ideological system, one can accept or reject the Hitlerian ideology – that is a matter of political opinion. But everyone will understand that one cannot destroy an ideology by force. It is therefore not only senseless but criminal to embark on such a war – a war for the destruction of Hitlerism disguised as a battle for democracy."'

The Americans were also very tough. Secretary of State John Foster Dulles began his speech at the NATO conference of December 1958 by referring to the ultimatum as the first concrete threat since the Berlin blockade of 1948–9. 'Moscow has started a war of nerves, as could be seen from the Soviet note of 13 December, delivered on the eve of the NATO conference. But the Soviet Union should realize that the United States could wipe her out just as easily as Russia could wipe out Europe. The USA has more powerful deterrents than the Soviet Union. Therefore it is an empty threat, a test of Western resistance, comparable to the contempt shown by Hitler for responsible advice.'

But scarcely a month later, in January 1959, Khrushchev had another bright idea: he submitted a scheme for a German Peace Treaty. The state of war with Germany was to be ended, the two German States released from their respective military alliances, and neutralized and controlled by the two Superpowers. Berlin would be a third independent entity. There was to be a confederation within a European security

74

system – this was dangled as a bait promising eventual re-unification. But the devil's hoof was so clearly visible that no one showed much interest in this new scheme. For the next four years the Berlin crisis that had begun with Khrushchev's speech in the Moscow Stadium was to keep Bonn and the three Western Powers in a state of breathless suspense; then the Cuban crisis came along and overshadowed everything else.

But gradually certain differences of opinion began to appear between the Federal Republic and her allies. Bonn's policy of immobility began to get on everyone's nerves. The Opposition in the Federal Assembly had been irritated by it for a long time. In January 1958 a debate of unwonted violence on foreign policy took place in Bonn dealing with George Kennan's ideas for disengagement, put forward in his famous series of Reith lectures; the so-called Rapacki Plan put forward by the Polish Foreign Minister Adam Rapacki; and other projects for a European zone free from atomic weapons. The most savage attacks came from Thomas Dehler of the FDP and from the future Federal President Gustav Heinemann. Heinemann had resigned as CDU Home Secretary in 1950 in protest against Adenauer's rearmament policy, and now sat in the Assembly as a member of the SPD.

By this time the Allies were beginning to grow impatient too. Washington's toughest anti-Communist, John Foster Dulles, had rejected Kennan's containment policy in favour of a roll-back policy: but now, towards the end of his life, even he had reached the conviction that at the best Communism could be damned, but never rolled back. It is said that on his last visit to Bonn in February 1959, shortly before his death, he announced to Adenauer that from now on the United States would see whether a policy of *détente* would not be more successful than their policy of strength had been. This change of course became the policy of the new President John F. Kennedy. Adenauer was unable to go along with it. He kept asking the Americans to declare their loyalty to the Atlantic Pact and stuck to his self-created dogma.

The partners now decided to use the Berlin crisis as pretext for discussing the German question in depth, including the Oder-Neisse Line. The Western Allies' attitude to Germany's Eastern frontier had been laid down in the Potsdam Agreement of July 1945: 'The Heads of the three Governments confirm their view that the final demarcation of Poland's Western frontier should be deferred until the Peace Conference.' The Members of the German Federal Assembly had solemnly undertaken to solve this question without recourse to force; and on 20 October 1953 the Federal Chancellor had reaffirmed the undertaking.

In the spring of 1959 de Gaulle was the first to abandon this position. He said that the natural fate of the German people ought to be reunification with freedom within the present German frontiers. Many Germans agreed with him. My own point of view was this: 'A frontier compulsorily drawn between two peoples by a third power can never be trusted by the two ... The frontier between Poland and ourselves must be agreed between us: it must not be imposed by a third party. For years we have campaigned in *Die Zeit* for the resumption of diplomatic relations with Poland, and for closer contact between our two peoples. Much could be different today if only Bonn had adopted these ideas in time.'

Theodor Heuss's term of office as Federal President was due to end in September 1959. At eighty-three Adenauer too needed to think about a successor. The Party was sworn to support Ludwig Erhard, the architect of the economy, to the Chancellorship, but Adenauer had always been sceptical – and possibly jealous – of Erhard and was determined to prevent his candidature at any price. It was for this reason that he first suggested Erhard for the Federal Presidency. Then, early in 1959, he declared that he himself wished to take that office, but soon after changed his mind because, he said, he was indispensable as Chancellor. This wavering cost him a good deal of his reputation and marked the beginning of the decline of Federal Chancellor Adenauer. From now on until his resignation in October 1963 very little went right for him. And what was worse, he reacted unsatisfactorily to the great Russian challenge of 13 August 1961, when they began to build the Berlin Wall.

The atmosphere had been strained for some time; unrest could be felt, foreboding was in the air. On 4 August 1961 I wrote an article in *Die Zeit* which gives a better picture of the disquiet than one could paint today. It was headed: 'German Michel Sleeps':

Last week 150,000 reservists were called up in the USA because of the situation in Berlin. President Kennedy made a great speech in which he said: 'I am aware that many American families bear the burden of this call-up. Many people's careers and studies will be interrupted, husbands and sons will be called up, and in some cases people's incomes will be affected. But these are burdens we must bear if freedom is to be defended.'

No such words were heard in the Federal Republic, although the Berlin question concerned us more than anyone else. The Bonn response to John F. Kennedy's speech was gratitude to the Americans for their firm stand and a sense of relief: if 'those Americans' put their foot down then we won't have to worry, then everything will be all right...

It is sad: while our historical fate is being decided the people are asleep like the disciples at Gethsemane. Then, the spirit was willing but the flesh was weak. Today it seems to be the other way around: the flesh is powerful, but the spirit is weak.

Did we really survive under the ruins of the collapsing Reich in order to read balance sheets, and snuggle down in a corner of our homeland – if you can call it a homeland – surrounded by period furniture, garden gnomes, and Volkswagens?

Have we really become a people without a history, a people whom no vision has the power to shake out of its torpor, not even the image of the lost Eastern regions or a country divided into two states? Two states that have as little in common now as Holland and Belgium – who also were once an entity? Can this have happened to us, a people to whom history spoke so clearly?

The Germans represented a whole generation when they enacted their play in the heart of Europe, a play in which primeval heathenism and modern science and technology formed a blood-curdling combination. Cold shivers ran down the spines of the spectator nations as they contemplated the image of man on the German stage. Finally the actors themselves were struck down by a hailstorm of bombs and drowned in rivers of blood: the silence of death gradually spread over Germany. And then the Soviets broke in from the East and satisfied their greed and grabbed whatever they could.

And the nation was divided in two, and one half was humiliated and enslaved. The victors presented a slogan to the other half: good speed to the able and the efficient. And the able and efficient did very well: bank accounts grew larger, the economy became increasingly concentrated, size and numbers ruled everywhere. Each year's figures exceeded those of the previous year: the growth rate doubled, three times as many people travelled abroad, there were four times as many books at the Frankfurt Fair, five times as much beer was drunk at the Munich Beer Festival . . . but repletion did not produce insight or wisdom.

Nobody thinks about Germany's history during the past twenty-five years. And now? What next? How many people are kept awake by that question? Alas, they all sleep only too well!

A week later, on 13 August, the radio announced that Russian troops were massing in Berlin. I rang up my colleague Theo Sommer; we both caught the next plane to Berlin and saw the GDR soldiers putting up barbed wire along the sector frontier in preparation for the Wall.

In Bonn there was general panic. Even NATO had evidently not anticipated this form of Eastern provocation among all the other possible forms it might have taken. But the most astonishing thing was that next day Adenauer started on his pre-arranged electoral tour of Bavaria as though nothing had happened. And many people were indignant that in his election speeches he was not ashamed to slander Willy Brandt, the ruling SPD Mayor of the beleaguered city, and did not even refrain from referring to Brandt's illegitimate birth.

For three days a British European Airways plane chartered by the CDU stood ready at Wahn airport to take the Chancellor to Berlin. But even during the following days he could not make up his mind to leave. 'It would only help Brandt', he is supposed to have said. It was nine days before he flew to the former capital of the Reich, a city he had never liked and where his reception – unlike Vice-President Lyndon Johnson's who had preceded him – was distinctly cool. He had no sense of the nation's shock, no heart, no political instinct, and he paid for it in the next elections to the Federal Assembly.

Before these events no one had doubted that the CDU/CSU would once again have an absolute majority. But when the votes were counted the Party had lost twenty-nine seats and with them its absolute majority. The FDP reacted with the slogan, 'Never again an FDP Minister in an Adenauer Cabinet!' The liberals wanted to put in Erhard as Chancellor, but Adenauer was not yet weak enough to allow that. He was not yet thinking of retiring. This time, however, he was forced to commit himself – and commit himself in writing – to staying only two years longer.

The coalition talks after the 1961 election turned out to be extraordinarily difficult, because the election results had gone to the head of the FDP, who had done better than any other party. They kept making fresh demands; among other things they wanted FDP Secretaries of State or Ministers of State (in other words, watchdogs) in the Ministries of Home Affairs, Foreign Affairs, and Finance. The talks lasted for nearly two months, and the result even then was a pretty shaky government. The cabinet was rent with discontent, squabbles, jealousy, and insubordination, and the Chancellor kept it under-informed or not informed at all.

In mid-October, even before the government was formed, Foreign Secretary von Brentano resigned. He had realized that the FDP who were in favour of greater flexibility would hamper CDU foreign policy if the Foreign Secretary in office had an FDP Minister of State looking over his shoulder. Besides, after serving the Chancellor for so many years as faithfully as a vassal to his feudal lord, Brentano felt that he had been left in the lurch, and the Chancellor quite evidently seemed ready to sacrifice him to satisfy the FDP.

A year later another catastrophe cast a shadow over the Chancellor's image. Right in the middle of the Cuban crisis the *Spiegel* affair triggered off a major government crisis in Bonn. On 19 November the five FDP Ministers resigned. On 27 November the CDU/CSU members of the cabinet followed. On 14 December Adenauer's last cabinet – now without Franz Josef Strauss – was sworn in. What had happened?

On 10 October 1961 *Der Spiegel* carried a story about the NATO autumn manœuvres which included material from a Defence Ministry report classified as secret. The article was headed 'Conditionally Prepared for Defence', and said that the manœuvres had persuaded the Ministry that the *Bundeswehr* was too weak to defend the country. It needed to be bigger and armed with medium-range rockets.

One's first reaction was to assume that military secrets had been betrayed. But the court in Karlsruhe later established that all the information contained in the article had already been published piecemeal in various other papers, and that it would have been possible without any knowledge of the secret report to piece together a mosaic leading to the same conclusions as the article in *Der Spiegel*.

But Defence Minister Franz Josef Strauss had not the patience to wait for this verdict. *Der Spiegel* had often dealt badly with him, and he regarded it as his arch-enemy. So he started proceedings against the culprits. He ordered the Military Attaché in Madrid to have Franco's police arrest Konrad Ahlers, the deputy chief editor of *Der Spiegel* who was on holiday in Spain. For a long time, even in the Assembly, Strauss denied that he had done this.

When the truth was finally known, everyone regarded it as an act of personal revenge on Strauss' part. The people were suitably indignant: after thirteen years of CDU rule the press was their mutual ally against arbitrary behaviour by the State. And the State prosecutors had acted with the lightning speed having police surround the *Spiegel* offices in the Hamburg's

Press House as though it were a terrorist hide-out; the editors were turned out of their rooms and even the archives and telephone exchange were cordoned off. The Federal Chancellor, possibly in order to shield Strauss, allowed himself to be carried away into making untenable statements: the execution order on the *Spiegel* had been necessary, he said, because the paper was 'a hotbed of treason'. So the suspects were sentenced before they had even been accused.

Never since the war had the German public been so stirred as by this affair. There were mass protests, because people were indignant about the attack on the freedom of the press, about careless accusations, about a Minister telling lies, and about the premature condemnation of the alleged culprits by the Head of State. The atmosphere at the time may be judged by an article headed 'The Spiegel Affair' that I wrote in *Die Zeit* of 16 November:

> No, and no again. This is not how we imagined the new Germany. The men who rebuilt and led the new Germany, one would have thought, would have more seriousness and integrity, and an acute awareness of their responsibility, as well as of the historical perspective. But this – no!
>
> The picture revealed in the last few days and weeks is horrendous. Is there anyone with values higher than his own point of view, his own aims, urges, or desires? The higher up you get in the hierarchy the rarer such people seem to be.
>
> The Chancellor puts the coalition first, because it guarantees his rule, and he believes that he alone can steer the Federal Republic through these troubled times. And with this sacred end in view, all means seem justifiable to him. . . .
>
> And the Minister of Defence? For a fortnight he left the world guessing who could have been responsible for Konrad Ahlers' arrest in Spain, while he stuck to his assertion, 'I have nothing to do with the whole business', in the truest sence of the words. But then, driven into a corner in the Assembly, he had to admit that he personally made the crucial telephone call to the military attaché, Colonel Oster in Madrid. But he too left his Secretary of State to carry the can. . . . Just imagine: a minister stays on and lets the Secretary of State who shielded him take the rap. What

sort of conditions do we live in? How was it possible for such a style of government to spread?

There is a story about a senior civil servant in the old Prussia. As he lay dying someone asked him what he was thinking about. Fully conscious he answered, 'About the State.' In those days the State was not regarded as an arrangement created by necessity and considerations of usefulness, but as a strange interaction between divine revelation and human conceptions.

But today, who thinks of the State at all? Who cares about its institutions at a time when everything revolves around individual safety, prosperity, and personal happiness? At a time when the standard of living has become the be-all and end-all of life?

Civics have been introduced into the school curriculum as a subject, but in the highest places there is little civic sense. The Minister for Home Affairs is also the Minister for the Constitution; and when this man was cornered in the Assembly he excused himself by saying that the Federal authorities who had Ahlers arrested in Spain had perhaps 'acted somewhat outside the bounds of legality'. It is the idea that democratic rules of play and formally demarcated paths may be all very well for mere subjects, but the leaders do not need to observe them because they can find their way without directions. If you have a friend with good contacts in the Spanish police, well, then you ring him up: it's so much simpler than wading through bureaucratic red tape.

'The more power a man holds in his hands, the greater his obligation to keep the rules', so the Federal Chancellor instructed *Der Spiegel*. But he himself in his limpid innocence apparently seems quite unaware of the power in his hands and the responsibility that goes with it. 'I don't have much respect for people who are always advertising in *Der Spiegel*', he announced. One firm replied with a telegram of protest, 'Is the freedom of advertising to be restricted?' and another, 'We won't let Adenauer intimidate us with his arguments'.

And furthermore: in their civics lessons people are taught that a person on remand is innocent until his guilt is proved in a court of law. But in the Assembly the Chancellor spoke of a publication 'that systematically commits treason in order to make money' thereby suggesting that Rudolf Augstein has been convicted and legally sentenced for treason and bribery. And then, 'If Ahlers had happened to be in Germany, the same fate would have overtaken him, it is therefore immaterial whether he was arrested in Malaga or in Hamburg. Let no one get worked up about that.' That remark does not exactly suggest that the Chancellor loses much sleep with scruples over whether the State is acting legally. Whether legitimately in Hamburg or 'somewhere outside the bounds of legality' in Spain an arrest is an arrest, and that is that. This lapidary way of thinking is typical of him and his regime.

The *Spiegel* affair provided a public test for the new Federal German democracy. The citizens passed it with flying colours; their immediate reaction was to stand up against the government's high-handed behaviour. The government, on the other hand, unfortunately failed the test. Twenty years have now gone by, and if we ask ourselves whether they have learnt better, then I think the answer is an unqualified yes.

Adenauer's fifth cabinet in 1962-3 was cobbled together from the debris of the fourth, but it presented no better picture. The Chancellor's authority had begun to crumble in 1959, and there was no way of stopping the rot: there were endless battles between the coalition partners. So there was a general sigh of relief when the head of government changed in October 1963: Adenauer remained head of the Party, but he left the Chancellory where he had ruled for fourteen years, and Ludwig Erhard moved in.

However conscious one is of Konrad Adenauer's great services to the country, it is impossible not to regard him with a mixture of admiration and aversion.

He was an almost frighteningly unapproachable man with no friends – at least if you take friendship to mean that confidence and intimacy are taken for granted. Perhaps he was too suspicious or too conceited. John Foster Dulles and Charles de Gaulle are frequently cited as friends, but in both cases friendship included a good deal of expediency. Possibly the banker Robert Pferdmenges was a real friend to the Chancellor, but his real human interest and warmth he reserved for his family.

All his close collaborators agree that in the long run you could only keep his esteem by being useful and ready to knuckle under. This fact, combined with his natural mistrustfulness, which in the course of his life developed into a genuine contempt for humanity, made friendship impossible, especially as he felt no need to discuss things or to clear his own ideas and test his arguments in conversation with others. For he himself knew what was best at any given moment as well as what was right in the long run, and other people's views did not interest him.

Arnulf Baring writes: 'If he thought it would work he would show ill-humour at the beginning of a conversation in order to intimidate his partner. But if it was a matter of winning someone over and making himself liked, then the Chancellor was capable of captivating charm and friendliness, spiced with jokes and flattery. When he had made up his mind to be charming he showed the most delicate attentiveness, even a positively touching politeness which seemed to come from the heart. He sent bouquets and postcards when he was on holiday; he pretended to take self-important characters into his confidence and asked insignificant politicians for their advice.'[33]

But how pitiless he could be to faithful friends who were dependent on him! No one had to endure as much as Foreign Secretary von Brentano. Baring published the correspondence between Adenauer and Brentano during the years 1949–64, and wrote a commentary in which he describes Brentano's resignation:

'Brentano really repaid trust with trust. As in feudal times he always regarded himself as a liegeman – a reliable vassal, the truest of the true; he endured Adenauer's frequently domineering thoughtlessness and bore many humiliations because he believed that to make up for all these wrongs the Chancellor's heart really belonged to him. When he recognized his mistake, when he noticed that loyalty was not repaid with loyalty, but that he was simply a colleague, a Foreign Secretary always at the Chancellor's disposal – then the ground began to tremble beneath his feet. With a few cold, unfeeling words spoken in public, Adenauer destroyed the human basis of Brentano's political life. After this moment of truth there was nothing left for Brentano but quietly to resign.

Adenauer behaved quite differently to Hans Globke who was Secretary of State in the Federal Chancellor's Office from 1953. During the Third Reich, Globke had had an important position in the Ministry for Home Affairs: together with his chief, Secretary of State Stuckart, he had written the commentary on the Nuremberg laws which codified the Nazi's racial ideology. Globke's supporters say that he exercised a softening influence, and also that he needed a cover because he was the confidential agent of the Catholic clergy: it was his job to keep the episcopal office in Berlin informed of the regime's plans and measures. As the opposition to Adenauer grew, Globke came increasingly under fire. He himself offered his resignation several times, but Adenauer would not let him go. He kept him through thick and thin because Globke was absolutely indispensable to him. In March 1961 Theodor Eschenburg wrote about him in *Die Zeit*: 'The Federal Chancellor's Office has become an instrument of control for the Chancellor, and, what is more, it is adequately efficient. It sees that the Chancellor's directives are really accepted, makes sure that they are observed, and co-ordinates the frequently divergent policies of the various ministries and their sometimes excessively stubborn ministers: all this is in large measure due to Globke.'

So Adenauer put up with all the suspicion and all the reproaches in connexion with the anti-Semitic laws that came his colleague's way, because the latter was useful to him. And yet Adenauer was the most uncompromising of all the German politicians on the question of Israel. With all his might he supported the reparations agreement with Israel that was signed on 10 September 1952, and from which by the end of

1980 the State of Israel has received 3.45 billion DM, and 70 billion has been paid in individual compensations.

One of Adenauer's greatest qualities was patience: he knew that everything needs time to mature. The maxims on which he acted were quite lapidary; and so the proverbs he was fond of citing were of an elementary, positively paterfamilias type of simplicity: 'Slow but sure'; or 'A man of few hopes is rarely disappointed'.

He was not a martyr to the pale cast of thought. Adenauer never questioned himself. In that period of new beginnings, the exhausted, disillusioned and deeply disturbed Germans needed a father figure, someone utterly to be relied on, and this patriarch who stuck imperturbably to what he had once recognized as right was a heaven-sent head of government for them. Nowadays everyone knows best, and most people are only prepared to tolerate their own opinions: at such a time Konrad Adenauer would be out of place and utterly lost.

So in the fourth decade of the Federal Republic its founder has already become an almost mythical figure. A relic of those legendary days, quite overgrown with anecdotes, he looms over our bureaucratic, technological world: a primeval political rock, as Herbert Wehner once called him.

4

Ludwig Erhard

Ludwig Erhard became Federal Chancellor on 16 October 1963. But his chancellorship was not to be the summit of his political career: it was a disappointing period for him and for the electorate as well. Konrad Adenauer had always predicted this, though of course it could have been a self-fulfilling prophecy. Adenauer had repeatedly said that it would be a mistake to put Erhard at the head of the government because he was totally unsuited to such a position: these warnings must surely have contributed to Erhard's sense of insecurity. The simple truth is that during his period of office Erhard's reputation began to fade. Not his historical reputation: that is assured; but in the public imagination the picture of a weak Chancellor gradually replaced that of an outstanding economic leader.

Strangely enough it soon became apparent that Erhard had no talent for decision-making, yet after the war it was he who had taken what was perhaps the hardest decision of all – and he took it against violent opposition from the SPD, from some members of the CDU, and from all the Occupying Powers. In those days, immediately after the currency reform, the important question was whether to go for a planned economy or a market economy. In spite of widespread scepticism among the general public and strong opposition from the Economic Council, Erhard did not hesitate to implement his faith in a market economy without ever wavering from it.

Erhard often spoke of the element of chance in his life. If you define chance as a kind of serendipity, then it is not surprising that Erhard found it so easy to make his economic decision. In order to understand this one needs to examine his career.

Like Henry Kissinger, Ludwig Erhard was born in Fürth near Nuremberg. He was destined to take over his father's textile business. A severe wound in the First World War put him out of action for several years. He was still convalescing in 1919, and in order not to waste this period of leisure, he enrolled at the newly-founded school for business studies in Nuremberg. 'This apparently insignificant decision', he later declared, 'proved to be a turning-point of far-reaching importance'. Having developed a taste for economics he felt an urge to extend his knowledge, fostered by his observation of Germany's problems. He went to the University of Frankfurt and worked for his degree under Franz Oppenheimer.

Although the causes and course of the First World War were quite different from those of the Second, the consequences for Germany were very similar. The Treaty of Versailles with its ludicrous reparation demands led to steadily accelerating inflation as more and more money was printed. Exports went down. The servicemen who had been unemployed since their return from the front seemed increasingly likely to be a source of potential unrest. In December 1921 Germany asked for a moratorium on reparations payments, but Poincaré, the head of the French government, would not agree to it. In January 1923, when Germany finally found herself unable to continue paying, 40,000 French soldiers supported by Belgian units were sent into the Ruhr to occupy mines and factories. In the very first few days workers were killed defending their place of work, the Krupp complex. Everywhere resistance was broken by force. Protests by Britain and the USA went unheeded. The French company, Mission Interalliée de Controle des Usines et Mines, was given a free hand to exploit the region.

The population countered by means of passive resistance. All the railways in the Ruhr stopped; the trams ceased to run, not a smoking chimney was to be seen. The deaths columns in the newspapers were full of announcements about people who had 'died in the battle of the Ruhr'. More than 100,000 were driven from their homes, and the prisons were full. This situation continued until October – but a complete French withdrawal took place only years later.

Meanwhile paralysis and poverty gnawed away at the country. Industrial production had almost ceased, the currency was totally devalued: wages paid on Saturday were worth only half by Monday. The entire middle class had suddenly been dispossessed: all their savings, insurance policies and pensions had lost their value. Anyone with a little foreign currency could buy whatever they wanted – works of art, houses, land, jewellery – all the things that the new poor were forced to sell in order to stay alive. The effect on the nation was xenophobia, anti-Semitism, and extremism of the right and left.

Finally on 15 November 1923 the mark was stabilized. The new mark was guaranteed by a mortgage on all agricultural and industrial assets. And the Dawes Plan solved the reparations question on a purely economic basis with all elements of revenge eliminated.

The economic collapse, the ruin of the currency and the stabilization that followed were fundamental experiences for Erhard's understanding of economics. In 1928 he joined the Institute for Economic Research at Nuremberg that had been founded as an extension to the business school he had attended. Once more, in the early 1930s, when unemployment had risen to six million and families had to manage on a dole of 20 RM a week, he was able to observe the correlation between economic misery and political extremism. By the end of that period there were only Communists and Nazis: the centre had simply been eaten away.

For the next fourteen years Erhard worked on market research in the newly-founded institute and thus acquired an extensive personal knowledge of who was who on the economic and industrial scene. He also had every opportunity of studying the role of psychological factors in economics. Both these experiences were to prove very useful in the years after the Second World War. The war was still in progress in 1943 when Erhard started working on a memorandum entitled 'Financing Wars and Consolidating Debts'. It was three hundred pages long and made no bones about assuming that the war would be lost and plans needed for the period after Hitler. In official Nazi-speak such thoughts were defeatism punishable by death.

In those days Erhard and Karl Blessing (later to become President of the Federal Bank) would often meet Professor Theodor Eschenburg at the house of Erhard's brother-in-law, Karl Guth. The Professor remembers an episode which is typically Erhard. One night in the autumn of 1944, about two months after the attempt on Hitler's life, when the group were sitting together, Erhard suddenly dug into the huge shapeless briefcase he always carried about with him and fished out one of the many pamphlets it contained. This he presented to Eschenburg with the words, 'For you alone'. It was a précis of the memorandum.

Eschenburg read it the same night and says it filled him with admiration, but even more with fear. He decided to return the pamphlet as fast as he could. Making his way through the attic that linked their two flats, he knocked on Erhard's door. It was a long time before he managed to wake him. Eschenburg returned the exposé with a few words of thanks and admiration, and said he did not want to keep it any longer because if it were found in a house search whoever had it in his possession would certainly be arrested. 'And is that why you've woken me up?' Erhard said grumpily and took back his paper.

The next evening Eschenburg met him by chance at the Potsdamer station. Erhard was carrying his bulging briefcase. Eschenburg asked whether he was still humping the dangerous exposé around with him. Erhard silently opened the case: the contents were exactly the same as on the previous night. Not only did Erhard carry the pamphlet about, he had also sent it to a few like-minded experts in order to test their reactions. One of these had been Goerdeler, who was executed after the attempt on Hitler's life on 20 July 1944. But fortunately in this case Goerdeler seems to have been more careful than Erhard: the memorandum did not fall into the hands of the police; later, however, it did fall into the hands of the Americans, and this turned out to be the second lucky break in Erhard's life because it made the Americans sympathetic to the brave author of this far-sighted essay.

In 1947 the Economic Council of the British and American Occupation Zones, referred to as the Bizone, met for the first time at Frankfurt, which now became the centre of the Bizone. The Economic Council was a kind of parliament with no political power, but it had a certain number of important economic functions. Its 52 delegates, soon increased to 104, were elected by the assemblies of the different *Länder*. Apart from this 'parliament' there was an administrative Council – in effect a provisional German government. It consisted of a director-in-chief and five directors in charge, respectively, of the different departments.

Ludwig Erhard who shortly before had spent a few months as Minister for Economic Affairs in Bavaria now became the chairman of a group of currency and financial experts in the Economic Council. In September 1947 he went to Bad Homburg, where he was to run a special department on money and credit which was to prepare the currency reform. The Allied Control Commission had made two conditions in respect of currency reform: firstly, the plan was to include all four Occupation Zones; and secondly, before being put to the Germans it was to have the blessing of all the Allies. The first condition was well meant, but soon after Erhard had delivered the plan in January 1948, the Allied Control Commission in Berlin split up. The writing had been on the wall for some time: there was no longer any kind of unity between East and West as far as the administration of Berlin was concerned.

The end of collaboration came on 19 March 1948, when Marshal Sokolovsky, the Moscow representative on the

Allied Control Commission, left a joint meeting under protest. The next step was to move Berlin's city council from the Soviet to the British sector. On 24 June the Soviets used the currency reform issue as an excuse for closing all access to Berlin, by land as well as by water, so that the inhabitants received no supplies whatever. Moscow hoped that by these means she would force the Allies to retreat from the former capital. But General Clay and the British foiled her plan by arranging an air lift to bring supplies into the city: they kept it up for eleven months until the Russians abandoned their blockade on 12 May 1949.

Since March 1948 Erhard had been Director of Economic Administration, the most important department in the Administration Council. His appointment was due to the third and undoubtedly the most important stroke of fortune in his political career. And not merely in his career, but also in the existence of the Federal Republic, for she owes her present political position first and foremost to her economic status, and it was Ludwig Erhard who laid the foundations for that.

Early in January 1948 his predecessor, Johannes Semler, a leading member of the CSU, had made a most disgruntled and bad-tempered speech at Erlangen, in which he criticized the Americans for sending nothing but maize and chicken food to the starving Germans. Semler said the Germans could stop being grateful, because they had no cause whatsoever for gratitude. This speech made the Americans very indignant because they had been enormously generous – as had the British at a time when it was very hard for them to be so. One speaker declared that to date the Germans had received not only 750,000 tons of maize, but also 3.2 million tons of grain and half a million tons of other foodstuffs, at a total cost of 500 million dollars.

Semler had to go. At that time people could be appointed to positions without having to belong to any particular party, and Erhard, who did not yet belong to a party, was likely to meet the least opposition, and he was already very acceptable to the Americans. So he became Semler's successor. True, he only received forty-eight votes at his election; forty-nine delegates returned blank votes, and seven did not turn up. The SPD were against him to a man, and several members of the CDU – Adenauer not excepted – maintained an extremely sceptical attitude towards him. His majority was not exactly imposing, but at least the right man was now in the right place.

As early as the end of 1947 the Americans had printed money for the Germans and secretly shipped it in from the USA. It was kept under lock and key at one of their bases. While Erhard and his team were feverishly working on their plan for currency reform at Bad Homburg, the Americans for their part had given the same task to a highly able young Harvard specialist in finance and currency called Edward Tenenbaum. Although Tenenbaum had been born in the USA, he was of German parentage. He produced the Dodge–Colm–Goldsmith study on which the American plan was based. In mid-April 1948 under conditions of the strictest secrecy, the German team was flown to an American air base near Kassel where the American plan was revealed to them: each new currency unit was to be worth ten of the old. Thirty-five per cent of all existing savings were to be written off completely. Erhard had planned to share the burden equally, in order not to favour unduly those with concrete assets, but he was unable to make the Allies accept this proposition.

Meanwhile the economy had run even further aground. The bureaucracy and machinery of administration kept growing, with innumerable decrees, rules, and a bewildering multitude of permits; at the same time the quantity of goods to administer kept diminishing. In the end there was nothing left to administer but the lack of things. Everyone was hungry. Everything was at a standstill. Only inflation kept moving forward. From my window in the Warburgstrasse in Hamburg I could see two dustbins. The Swedish Consul General lived in the house where I rented a room, so all day long there was a succession of figures rummaging about in the dustbins for remains of food and cigarette butts.

At last on 19 June the day had come. The new currency was distributed. Each individual received 40 DM at the same rate as the old RM; businesses were given 60 DM per employee at the same one-to-one rate. Bank and savings bank deposits were later valued at 6.50 DM per 100 RM. Altogether it is estimated that about 40 billion RM was destroyed. The money supply was only increased gradually as production, and therefore supply, increased.

Before all this happened there had been months of endless, passionate discussion as to what should be done after the currency reform. Erhard expressed his view in many speeches: the whole currency reform would be pointless unless immediately afterwards the administration got rid of all permits, restrictions, and fetters. There should be only one kind of purchase permit, he said, namely money. Apart from a few restrictions he wanted to abolish all price controls and rationing. Unless this were done the will to achieve would be killed and shortages perpetuated. Everyone was sick of controls: they had resulted in a total lack of goods, since no one was prepared to exchange either goods or labour for money. All the same, no one could imagine how to get rid of the system. Only Ludwig Erhard was determined to do it at a stroke. He said there were only two alternatives: a free market economy or a return to a Hitler-style dictatorship. Moreover, in spite of warnings and in the teeth of general scepticism, he was convinced that following such measures production would automatically begin to rise.

In the spring of 1948 my editor sent me to Frankfurt. I found that the new Director for Economic Affairs, Ludwig Erhard, was to give a press conference that very day. I too had hardly heard of this man who was unknown to the public. Slightly late, I entered a barely furnished office. About a dozen journalists were sitting round a long table. At the top sat a man with a friendly baby face, tow-coloured hair and pale blue eyes. His head seemed to spring straight from his shoulders without any neck at all, which gave him a somewhat dumpy look. Whenever he drew on his cigar he was momentarily enveloped in a blue cloud which coincided exactly with an illuminating ray of sunlight, so that there was something mystical, or at any rate surrealist about his appearance. Thirty years later this image is still vividly before my eyes. But when I got back to my office I told my colleagues, 'If Germany were not already in ruins, this man with his absurd plan of abolishing all controls would certainly succeed in ruining her. Pray God he doesn't become Minister for Economic Affairs. After Hitler and the division of the country that would be our third catastrophe.' Like most people I could not imagine how one could possibly just get rid of all controls in a country where it was not even possible to buy a box of matches. For after all, your ration card still gave you certain, if meagre, rations. Each person was allowed 425 grammes of meat and 65 grammes of fat monthly at a guaranteed price of 10 RM; whereas in the open market half a kilo of butter – supposing you could find such a thing – cost 250 RM. Like all the other critics and doubting Thomases I was soon to discover that Erhard's radical treatment produced the promised results after a relatively short time.

In those days the thing I needed most was a suitcase because since I arrived on horse-back I had to put up with cardboard boxes. In a Hamburg shop I saw a magnificent leather suitcase, but it cost 400 DM. My salary at *Die Zeit* was 600 DM. Whether or not to buy the suitcase was therefore a major decision. By chance I ran into Hans Zehrer, a grand old man of journalism who was later to be editor-in-chief of *Die Welt* during its prime. I asked his advice. He gave it: 'It's obvious that the few remaining goods in the shops will soon have been sold; things can only keep getting dearer.' So I bought the suitcase. Incidentally, Zehrer was wrong. Far more goods than anyone supposed had been hoarded. True, even those would not have sufficed to satisfy the buying spree ahead if the Marshall Plan and other American loans had not helped to import consumer goods. As for my suitcase, in view of the gradually falling price of goods it certainly had been too expensive. But even if I had to tighten my belt for a while, the decision to buy it was the right one. The suitcase was indestructible. The last time it accompanied me was to Moscow in 1978, and in our thirty years together we must have travelled the equivalent of a dozen times round the globe.

Currency reform had now been decided. The second decision, on whether the next step should be a planned or a market economy, still lay ahead. Willi Schickling describes the decisive battle of words in the Frankfurt Economic Assembly in which market economy won the day against the stubborn opposition of the SPD.

From 9 am on 17 June 1948 until 5 am on 18 June, the Economic Assembly conference hall of the Frankfurt stock exchange witnessed the greatest battle of words in the history of the Combined Economic Zone. Ludwig Erhard and his friends and collaborators on the Economic Council knew what was at stake. Now or never economic policy would have to be set on a new course. It was absolutely essential for the economic reform to be carried out before the weekend, so that the new currency could succeed with fewer restrictions and in a gradually expanding free market. Erhard's speech was a passionate plea based on expert knowledge: he called on Germany to throw off the 'straitjacket' of a state controlled economy. He explained to the delegates that currency reform alone would not produce healthy economic and social conditions unless the economy and the policy on prices were to be allowed a freer development. He emphasized and urged that only free tough competition demanding strenuous efforts from every individual would help the German people and the German economy to emerge from their destitution. ....[35]

The opposition protested, 'What about the old, the sick, the weak?' One of the SPD speakers, Dr Kreyssig, said: 'In my view, to throw a mortally sick man into ice cold water is a highly dubious undertaking: and for three years the German economy has been mortally sick. What I and my group wish to emphasize above all else is that we consider it a dangerous measure to throw the patient into cold water at the very last moment, before there has been a chance to measure his pulse rate.' Another opposition delegate, Erwin Schoettle, argued: 'As we approach the dangerous bend which the German economy is bound to encounter after the currency reform, it sometimes seems to us that the ambition of certain gentlemen here is to take that bend at a speed of 120 km per hour and to put their foot down hard on the accelerator at the very moment of maximum danger ... The Social Democratic Party cannot go along with this attitude. For one thing, the drive to free the economy may mean that a considerable number of our people will be unable to keep up with the pace and will sink exhausted by the roadside.'

Erhard had always thought of his market economy as based on social concern, and not as a mere revival of unrestricted liberalism or of capitalism with the brakes off. At the end of this twenty-hour debate the decision was finally taken to implement it. But the consent of the Allies had still to be obtained. Erhard knew that they would never give it in the form he wished. So, that very same day, a Friday, he decided to create a *fait accompli.* It is well known that bureaucracies are unable to function over the weekend, and he was going to make good use of that. He announced that he would make a broadcast on Sunday 20 July telling the public that rationing would be ended, and at the same time he said that he intended immediately to make a certain number of consumer goods freely available. On Monday morning he was summoned to appear before an angry Allied Commission. The British were especially indignant; most of their own food was still rationed. The German Director for Economic Affairs was accused of having violated Allied rights and altered Allied economic directives. He replied, 'I did not alter them, I abolished them.'

When General Clay, the American head of the Control Commission, said that all his advisers were against it, Erhard replied, 'I can assure you, General, you're not alone. Mine are all against it too.' 'OK. I'm not an expert, but I have a feeling you're on the right track. So go ahead.'

The black market disappeared very soon, and consumer goods slowly began to make their appearance. Fortunately the Director for Economic Affairs had been able to prevent a compulsory distribution of goods in the preceding period. Now that these goods could be sold, people were able to accumulate at least small amounts of capital and to reinvest them. Wages and salaries were frozen, and certain prices still remained under control. All the same, not everything went smoothly. At first, because people started rationalizing their businesses, prices went up and unemployment increased. Erhard's opponents were triumphant. They proposed a vote of no confidence, and in November the unions called a twenty-four-hour general strike. But this did not change anything.

It was not until the first six months of the following year that Erhard's predictions began to come true. Prices dropped and production rose. The Berlin blockade had benefited Erhard by absorbing everyone's attention, and by the time it was over the market economy was firmly established.

Jacques Rueff, later de Gaulle's currency adviser, was enthusiastic about the West German currency reform. His memory is slightly defective in that the benefits of the policy took a little longer to appear than he remembers, but his figures are correct. He wrote at the time: 'From June 1948 onwards everything changed at a blow. All statistical curves started rising. Agricultural and industrial production awoke simultaneously. Buildings began to shoot from the ground. Soon German reconstruction was setting a pace that none of her neighbours could have imagined. In the years 1948–52 exports multiplied by six, and the gross national income rose by 50 per cent between 1948 and 1950. Overnight the shops filled up with goods and the factories began to work. One day the Germans were wandering aimlessly around their cities trying to rustle up a few miserable extras for their diet; the next day they concentrated on producing them. On the eve, their faces expressed despair; the day after a whole nation was looking hopefully into the future.'[36]

Under these circumstances Erhard soon became known in West Germany. Many considered him a miracle doctor. So the first elections to the Federal Parliament in the autumn of 1949 brought a vote for Erhard: for most people Konrad Adenauer was still an unknown quantity. A poll taken in 1949 showed Adenauer behind Ludwig Erhard and Kurt Schumacher, the leader of the SPD. If it had not been for Erhard, Schumacher would probably have been elected Chancellor. After all, the SPD was the oldest party and had won a reputation for its resistance to Hitler, whereas the CDU/CSU was newly founded and no one knew how it would turn out.

In 1963, Franz Josef Strauss, then the youngest member of the Economic Council, wrote an article for the *Deutsche Zeitung und Wirtschaftszeitung* in which he said: 'The decision of the electorate in 1949 to vote for the CDU/CSU was first and foremost a mandate for Erhard to continue on his path towards a socially responsible market economy.' Strauss concluded that but for Erhard 'the first Chancellor of the Federal Republic would have been not Adenauer, but Schumacher.'

In those days the burning problem closest to every politician's heart was the plight of the refugees. In 1945 twelve million refugees had poured into the Federal Republic. The *Länder* along the East German border from Schleswig-Holstein to Bavaria were hardest hit by the almost insoluble problem of housing and feeding all these people. They were quartered in empty POW camps, drill halls and other large buildings which had happened to escape the bombing. They had lost everything, while the people of West Germany had kept almost everything. There would have to be some kind of compensation, otherwise social tensions were bound to arise and the integration of the refugees into West Germany would become impossible.

When the Federal Republic was founded West Germany at last had a central administration, and the currency reform made it possible to evaluate the wealth of the West Germans. In 1949 an instant assistance law was passed. West German wealth was taxed at 5 per cent in order to obtain funds for the integration of the refugees. Three years later, in 1952, this provisional law was replaced by a compensation law. West German wealth – land, industry, and trade – was taxed at between 2 and 4 per cent depending on the type of property. Losses of the refugees up to 4800 DM were fully repaid in DM. After that losses were compensated on a sliding scale, with medium losses receiving considerably less, and major ones uniformly compensated at about 10 per cent with a maximum limit. Apart from this compensation for lost wealth there was also compensation for lost and diminished income. Refugees and sufferers from war damage were given loans for dwellings, to help them find work, for training, and for starting up in business. Up to 31 December 1971 the compensation fund from which these payments were made had absorbed 82.8 billion DM. Of this total, 67.5 per cent went to the refugees, 19.4 per cent to the disabled, 9.4 per cent to people who had lost their savings, 0.6 per cent for other losses, and 3.1 per cent to refugees from the GDR. Until the building of the Wall in 1961, 2.7 million refugees from the GDR had asked for asylum.

Moreover, article 131 of the Constitution obliged the Federation to provide suitably for all those members of the public service who had lost their rights and livelihood through the division of the Reich, through the liquidation of the army and the *Arbeitsdienst* (youth training schemes), or from some other cause. The same applied to retired public servants and those of their dependants entitled to support. By the end of 1968 these liabilities had absorbed 30 billion DM.

Never before has any country seen so vast a transfer of wealth. The efforts to ensure social justice are surely one of the reasons why there has never been large-scale social unrest in the Federal Republic, even though all the conditions for it were present. Having paid the 2 per cent levy on agricultural land, large properties were also subject to a special land reform. The Occupying Powers had decreed that owners of large estates should relinquish part of their holdings. If these were agricultural, and not forest, they were resettled. This was done mainly for political reasons in order, as the Allies said, 'to break the power of the great landowners'.

It was Erhard's economic policy that gave the CDU victory in the first election that took place on 14 August 1949. The CDU won 139 seats, the SPD 131 seats, and the FDP, the liberals, 52 seats. The KPD, the communists, got fifteen seats. At the next election in 1953, they polled only 2.2 per cent of the vote, and since there is a clause to the effect that no party with less than 5 per cent of the vote can claim a seat in parliament, they were therefore excluded and never entered the Bundestag again.

Four weeks later Adenauer was elected the first Chancellor of the Federal Republic, and Erhard took on the Ministry of Economic Affairs. In the course of the next few years the new Minister for Economic Affairs still had to continue his incessant battle for a market economy. Especially when the Korean war pushed up the cost of all raw materials (crude rubber rose by 350 per cent) there were always voices demanding a return to controls and a planned economy. Erhard, who had a great gift for presenting complicated ideas in a popular, easy manner, once said, 'You can't have a little bit of planned economy any more than you can be a little bit pregnant'. And he never tired of putting his point to the Opposition in Parliament. He used to insist that the desire for consumer goods was not a vice, as certain puritans made out. 'There *must* be expansion,' he said. 'There are people – probably a lot of them – who feel that to satisfy the demand for luxuries is something that does not fit into the present social landscape. Lots of people are angry at seeing so many beautiful cars and other valuable things. Taking a short-term view this is understandable. But to ban goods of this kind entails banning their production and losing the national income that depends on it. In economics there is no income that is not directly linked to the production of goods.'

Ludwig Erhard's demand was 'Prosperity for all'. So far as is humanly possible he attained his goal. Houses, flats, cars, luxury travel – these are no longer the monopoly of a few; they are enjoyed by the masses. But here too we can see that a sensible development rooted in a community of effort can easily run out of control if it simply keeps going in the same direction without ever stopping and thinking. In the present case Erhard's community of effort turned into a consumer society in which many people suffer from spiritual atrophy, and politicians and economists despair because they cannot stop the wheels. Now the citizen expects more each year: more wages, more leisure, more consumer goods.

When the elections for the second Federal Assembly were held in the autumn of 1953, it was once more Erhard's economic policy that the voters acknowledged; for in foreign affairs – Adenauer's domain – Germany still lagged far behind. No treaties had yet been signed, and the Federal Republic was still occupied. In economics, on the other hand, there had been much progress. This time the CDU/CSU therefore polled 12.5 million votes and the SPD barely 8 million.

A few facts and figures show what economic progress had been made. By 1953 half a million homes were being built annually. The monthly export figures rose from 300 million DM in 1949 to nearly 3 billion DM in 1956. Already in 1954 the Federal Republic had become the biggest steel producer in Western Europe. One year later there was full employment. By 1957, the Federal Republic had the largest gold reserves of any country in the world except the USA. By the end of 1958 when 30 per cent of the gross national product was being exported, the Deutschmark was fully convertible with an export turnover of nearly 70 billion DM.

In the spring of 1959 it turned out that the acting President Theodor Heuss would not be able to make a bid for a third term as President because of party political difficulties. Adenauer was by then eighty-one years old, so it was necessary to think of a new incumbent for the highest office in the land. As always on such occasions, there was a lot of pushing and shoving, front-line talk and behind the scenes motivation. Naturally the fiercest battle was within the CDU, because it was obvious that the decision about the presidency would affect the candidatures for the chancellorship in the 1961 elections to the Federal Assembly. So the main debate was on who would succeed Adenauer rather than who would succeed Heuss. Straw polls showed that 32 per cent were in favour of Erhard – all the other CDU members polled less than 10 per cent of the votes. Adenauer had always been sceptical about Erhard, and now he was determined to prevent the CDU from electing him Chancellor. So he launched the idea of pushing Erhard, who was also Vice-Chancellor, upstairs into the position of President. Adenauer's argument that Erhard knew nothing about foreign policy was absolutely true. But he must have forgotten that when he began his career after 1945 he too had hardly been an expert on foreign affairs.

As usual, Adenauer set about his plan in a crafty manner. First of all he persuaded a small, carefully composed group to back his idea. It consisted of four ministers and a few important citizens of Bonn. But when he marched this auxiliary force before the Assembly members, a mutiny broke out. Adenauer's power met its first check. The delegates had no difficulty in seeing what he was at, and they refused to sacrifice their popular Minister for Economic Affairs, on whom they were going to rely as a vote-catcher in the 1961 election.

So the general surprise was all the greater when early in 1959 Adenauer suddenly declared that he wanted to stand for President himself. There was general relief, and much praise for the wisdom of the grand old man although this was mixed with some suspicion that he might be intending to change the function of this ceremonial office and to use it as a base from which to control the Chancellor – who seemed likely to be Erhard. Two months later, in early June, Adenauer changed his mind. He didn't want to be President after all. There was a storm of indignation. It was the beginning of the end of Adenauer. His public reputation plummeted like a thermometer in a sudden cold spell. His authority within the party was shaken.

Anyone who thought that Konrad Adenauer would now try to obliterate the evidence of behaviour which had led to a serious crisis over the chancellorship was very much mistaken. Quite the contrary: he was still determined to attack the 'crown prince' whom he found such a nuisance; so he began once more to spread the rumour that Erhard was unpredictable in foreign affairs, and that therefore he himself, Adenauer, would have to remain Chancellor – because the situation was as serious as never before.

Erhard returned from a visit to Washington on 9 June and told journalists: 'It has been put that I am less steadfast and less clear in my foreign policy than the Federal Chancellor. Such an historic lie cannot be left to circulate; nor can the imputation that I am against European integration. I shall fight to have these lies withdrawn.' But it was not in Erhard's nature to fight an opponent like Adenauer, who was not above spreading further untruths. Adenauer also continued to give interviews in which he said that the Minister for Economic Affairs had no talent for foreign policy. Erhard defended himself, but he never attacked. Perhaps it was this, after all, which made him rise even higher in the public esteem, whereas Adenauer's popularity was undermined by his aggressive malevolence. An opinion poll taken after these events showed that 50 per cent wanted Erhard to be Federal Chancellor, and only 32 per cent still wanted Adenauer to continue in office.

The 1961 election result expressed the public reaction to this episode, as well as the fact that Adenauer had seemed unmoved when the Russians began to build the Berlin Wall in August 1961. Consequently the CDU lost twenty-nine of the seats it had gained in 1957. Adenauer was elected Chancellor, but was made to give a written undertaking to resign in time for the 1965 elections. However, before that date another serious quarrel loomed between him and Erhard.

It began in early 1963 when de Gaulle vetoed Britain's entry to the Common Market. During the crisis that followed at Brussels, Erhard opposed de Gaulle's view very firmly, while Adenauer tried hard to pass over the matter in silence. This man who had always been so far above criticism or applause was strangely humble in his behaviour towards de Gaulle: almost always he expressed agreement and admiration for the General's policy.

De Gaulle's relationship with the USA led to continued rows between Adenauer and Erhard. Adenauer's experience of world events went back to the nineteenth century, and he regarded the reconciliation of France and Germany as the most important element in his foreign policy. Erhard, on the other hand, recognized quite clearly that in the second half of the twentieth century a close link with the USA was essential, especially as the Soviet zone of influence now stretched as far as the Elbe. To characterize their respective positions Adenauer was sometimes called a 'Gaullist' and Erhard an 'Atlanticist'.

The two men had very different concepts of what Europe might be. From the very beginning Erhard had been critical of the Treaty of Rome. In 1957 he said, 'I cannot feign enthusiasm for this treaty, because although I approve of the content, I cannot approve the methods or the time scale, nor in particular, the many loopholes left for evasions. In spite of this I shall vote for the Treaty.'

While Adenauer was quite ready to recognize de Gaulle as the leader of the European continent, Erhard was not. He was altogether sceptical about the General's motives. He suspected that de Gaulle was trying to benefit his own country by protecting it from troublesome competition.

Erhard was a liberal Greater European. He disliked the institutionalized arrangement limited to six countries, especially as they were to erect a customs barrier between themselves and the rest of Europe. That is why he became a committed supporter of Britain's entry, especially after Macmillan had visited Bonn in the summer of 1960 and persuaded him of the seriousness of Britain's candidature. Erhard mistrusted the French *planification* missionaries and the bureaucracy he saw growing up in Brussels, all this 'European economic incest' as he called it.

Under these circumstances the Franco–German pact signed by Adenauer and de Gaulle at the Elysée palace on 22 January 1963 was bound to be a bone of contention. For with this treaty de Gaulle had succeeded in establishing a co-operative special relationship between the two governments on a level outside supranational and international institutions. And what was possibly even worse, the pact was signed at a time when it was already easy to see that the General did not intend to allow Britain to join the EEC. The bilateral treaty therefore strengthened French bargaining power at Brussels; and it could be interpreted as showing that Germany was adopting de Gaulle's anti-American stance.

Because of this not only Erhard, but many members of the Bonn Assembly insisted on adding a minute to the Treaty in which the Bonn government declared that it did not regard it as conflicting in any way with the Common Market or NATO, and that it was not intended to do so. This did much to allay the fears of the 'European' Europeans and also of the Americans. True, it annoyed de Gaulle, but he soon calmed down. In the summer he gave a dinner for members of the French Assembly at which he said, 'Treaties are like young girls and roses – *Ça dure que ça dure*'. If the Franco–German pact was never put to any practical use, he said, it would not be the first time such a thing had happened in the course of history.

De Gaulle's veto on British entry into the EEC not only had a long-term negative effect on Erhard's relations with France, but also decisively hindered the development of Europe. Today we hear many complaints from Brussels about the alleged egotism and obstructiveness of the British, but the root cause of all this is the decision taken in 1963. The British missed ten years of European progress, and those ten years in which the other nations developed simply cannot be made good. At the time of the breakdown in the negotiations I wrote an article in *Die Zeit* entitled 'A Black Day':

In the very middle of the twentieth century the virus of national self-importance has once again spread from ages long since past. Europe was just beginning to grow together into a community of interest, and now the old three-cornered game between England, France and Germany has been resurrected from among the moth-balls.

Good God! Europe has passed through two world wars in which the old ideas and rules of play were carried *ad absurdum*; then, with the help of the Americans, the pieces were picked up and reassembled to form a new pattern; and now we have two old gentlemen wanting to go back to the old game and play it according to the rules of the day before yesterday. And what is more, they think themselves exceptionally far-sighted and progressive. It is almost like a Greek tragedy: Konrad Adenauer imagines he is crowning the work of Franco–German reconciliation with his treaty, and never sees that in fact it undermines the foundations of European unity. He is exactly like the generals who are always making preparations for the last, not the next war. He is busy removing non-existent obstacles, quite unaware that meanwhile he has piled up the old rubbish to form impassable barriers.

For thirteen years Adenauer has patiently and consistently steered the Federal Republic towards the West and tied her up in that port, regardless of the possibility that reunification might – as some think – have been purchased at the cost of remaining neutral. He thereby showed that he valued membership of the Western community higher than the reunification of Germany: and now he sacrifices this community for the sake of his friendship with General de Gaulle. And he never sees that it is only the General, and not the French people, who is asking him to make this sacrifice. The people of France bear no feelings of vengeance towards the British.

At last, with 1963, the time had come. Until the very last moment Adenauer tried to sabotage Erhard's election to the chancellorship by inventing more and more new candidates. The election was hard fought, but finally the Party asserted its will: in October 1963 Adenauer undertook to make way for Erhard, who was just about to celebrate his sixty-seventh birthday.

On 17 October 1963 Erhard presided over his first Cabinet meeting. Michael Caro describes the change:

A minister who can be described as an expert since he served under both Federal Chancellors gave me the following description with the pros and cons between then and now: Adenauer was a genius of superficiality and a master of improvization. He understood the art of suddenly producing an effect with one or two remarks; possibly foolish ones, and even if what he had to say was far from profound. By this means he was able not only to change the course of an unpleasant debate, but also to steer a conversation towards the decision he desired.

Erhard is the exact opposite. Because of this, he is much more ready than Adenauer to discuss matters and listen to the other opinions on questions that seem debatable to him. Therefore the cabinet meetings under Erhard tend to be a little longer than before.

Adenauer was authoritarian in cabinet: he alone decided the scenario for each meeting. He treated his ministers like students in a seminar. There was never any real discussion among the ministers, except on the rare occasions when Adenauer himself was uncertain. Adenauer would always indulge in long soliloquies, especially if he was trying to get by without having to broach unpleasant items on the agenda; or when he wanted tricky problems to be dealt with as quickly as possible because of lack of time. When he returned from abroad he gave his ministers only very brief and general accounts of his conversations with foreign politicians. Sometimes they were barely more informative than reports in the press.

For Erhard, on the other hand, discussion is the primary process for forming political opinions. He speaks very freely to his ministers, even about diplomatic secrets. Even in his position as Federal Chancellor he is prepared to learn from others. For the first time since the foundation of the Federal Republic there is an atmosphere in cabinet of being among colleagues. The Ministers are better tempered than under Adenauer; for they regarded him as a strict schoolmaster who might be expected to produce a disagreeable surprise at any moment.[37]

Erhard's attitude to power was quite different from Adenauer's. Konrad Adenauer demanded complete loyalty to the point of self-abnegation from those who worked with him, and the more loyal they were the worse he treated them. He used power in an authoritarian way. To him leadership meant making the decisions because the authority was his. If it looked as though it might be difficult to get his own way along the normal chain of command, then 'the old man', as he was often affectionately known, had a large repertoire of ways and means. Lying – he called it 'extending the limits of truth' – was certainly the most primitive among them. There were others such as cracking jokes, manipulating people, collecting gossip and keeping dossiers not only on his enemies but on his friends as well. When the moment came he would use the knowledge he had acquired either to ask a question, or to make a veiled threat, or to launch an amusing or destructive quip: 'Herr B., I'm told you often go to Cologne for the evening. Does your wife know about this?'

Compared with Adenauer's Machiavellian arts Erhard was almost naive. He regarded power as a completely calculable factor with nothing mysterious about it, and he wanted as little to do with it as possible. He held the simplistic view that if he did not demonstrate his power, in fact, if he could deny its existence, then it could do no harm. Erhard was averse to everything authoritarian. He felt at home in a pluralist society. Discussion was essential to him and team work a matter of course. For him, to lead was to persuade, and he believed in persuasion because he believed that human beings act according to reason and their own best interests.

People had great expectations of Erhard as the new Federal Chancellor: a liberal following an arch conservative. But disillusion soon set in. Hopes of a completely new start were perhaps pitched too high: the young had hoped that after Adenauer's patriarchal regime a new era was about to dawn. Industry and business counted on a steady upswing. The intellectuals thought that it would mean the end of the Rhenish clique, and that a less parochial phase would begin. And the man in the street thought that now there would be no end to the economic miracle.

But as soon as Erhard began to form his government it became apparent that for reasons of coalition he was not going to be able to keep his promise of a smaller, leaner cabinet. The unequivocal style of government that many had hoped for did not appear, and some even missed the firm hand in whose grip they had so recently groaned.

The grounds for criticism were easy to see, but it must be said that Erhard's heritage was an encumbered and difficult one. Since 1959 Adenauer had ridden on a loose rein. Much had been left undone and there had been many failures. Relations with the USA had been increasingly under pressure. Relations with France grew more difficult too, because de Gaulle considered Erhard 'Anglophile' and was consequently suspicious of him. But worst of all was the fact that the German government was unable to prevent itself from being drawn into the growing tension between France and the USA. It made no difference that Bonn, of course, only wished to be equally friendly with both. It made no difference because de Gaulle and the Washington government held diametrically opposed ideas. Each of them needed the Federal Republic to realize its plans, so Bonn was under constant pressure to opt for one of them, which meant opting against the other.

Washington wanted Europe to 'speak with one voice', because she needed an effective partner. In Paris, on the other hand, de Gaulle never tired of proclaiming that he wanted complete national independence and was opposed to all systems that used terms like 'supranational', 'integration', or 'Atlanticism' to cloak the fact that they want to keep us in the grip of the familiar hegemony. He wanted a free hand for France to lead the Six. That was why he vetoed Britain's entry to the Common Market. He could never see that his concept of a Europe of 'fatherlands' must weaken rather than strengthen Europe's influence for the simple reason that it prevented her from presenting a united front.

Washington's military policy was in favour of a high atomic threshold and graded deterrents. De Gaulle, on the other hand, demanded a low atomic threshold and massive reprisals. Washington wanted NATO, Paris did not. Washington fought to keep the dollar (weakened by deficits in the balance of payments) as the leading world currency: de Gaulle called for a return to the gold standard, precisely to prevent such a thing. So their ends were different, and so were their means. They had only one thing in common: mutual distrust. 1969 was, according to the NATO treaty of 1949, the last date for a possible withdrawal from NATO, and the Americans feared that before that date de Gaulle would try to undermine the mutual defence pact to such an extent that it would break apart. The West European Six would then be an independent force under his leadership, with France being the only one among them with atomic weapons. De Gaulle for his part was unable to shake off the suspicion that the two Superpowers might decide once again to divide the world between them as they had at Yalta. Hence he wanted to create an independent Europe, a third force. But he went about it in the wrong way.

So Erhard found himself manœuvred into a dilemma which, as seen from Bonn, was both unpleasant and artificial. Meanwhile, the same tensions dominated the atmosphere within the Party. The greatest damage to the Chancellor's reputation was probably caused by the battle within the ranks of the CDU/CSU between the partisans of France and the USA respectively. Erhard could not manage to pull his party together. The main reason, of course, was that the conflict between the Gaullists and the Atlanticists was riven with personal feuds. Adenauer, for instance, complained that on de Gaulle's visit to Bonn in 1964 the general had not been treated with sufficient warmth. It was true that de Gaulle had sulked; but that was not because of his welcome – the great man cannot possibly have minded that – but because he felt the USA had the Federal Republic in tow.

On the home front it was the question of pensions that became Erhard's first stumbling-block – as it was later to be for Helmut Schmidt. There was a general desire to see pensions increased. Erhard was against a rise right across the board; instead, he wanted to give a spectacular increase to severely wounded ex-servicemen. In the past he had always inveighed against special interests and a democracy of favours; now this was to be where he took his stand. But he was not a match for the functionaries especially not in such a touchy area. The result was that some complained that he lacked toughness, and others that he had made the wrong psychological choice – in other words that he lacked political realism.

His first trip abroad also showed a lack of political realism. When de Gaulle received Federal Chancellor Erhard at the Elysée palace for the first time on 22 November 1963 Erhard realized he would not have an easy time with the French President. In July, before becoming Chancellor, he had said in an interview with the magazine *Paris Match*: 'De Gaulle needn't think I am going to make advances to him, I shall let him make the running. So far in the general's eyes I have been only a figure of the second rank. When I am Chancellor we shall be operating more or less at the same level. And then we shall be able to talk.' Nobody who knew de Gaulle could call this a very diplomatic statement.

His next important trip abroad was to the USA. In late December 1963 President Johnson invited Erhard to his farm in Texas. The contrast between this meeting and the rendezvous with de Gaulle was astonishing. The Federal Chancellor was over-enthusiastic at finding himself and the President in complete agreement: 'We see things in exactly the same way. We can open our hearts and souls to one another, and each can reveal his problems and difficulties ...' At a party on Johnson's ranch Texan exuberance and German songs combined to create an atmosphere of emotional exaggeration.

Everybody knows that even the best atmosphere is unable to change hard facts. Still, the improvement in German–American relations was genuine, and there was a very free exchange of views. Lyndon Johnson told the Federal Chancellor that he was tired of the Germans lecturing him on the danger of Communism. The Americans were fully aware of the danger themselves. He complained that every time the Americans mentioned so much as the possibility of discussing the Berlin question with the Soviets, the West Germans burst into 'shrieks of horror'. He asked Erhard to make some proposals himself. Erhard agreed. What he said sounded different from anything that had been said in Bonn during the Adenauer period. In those days every American attempt to lower the tension in the Cold War was automatically decried as a sell-out. But after Erhard's return to Germany little or nothing was done to put the American discussions into practice. That too was not untypical of the new Chancellor.

Moreover, the first two years of Erhard's Chancellorship were constantly overshadowed by two problems which on the face of it would seem peripheral: the MLF and the price of grain. Both were chiefly connected with France. The MLF, or Multilateral Force, was to be a project fleet of twenty-five ships each equipped with Polaris missiles and manned by crews of mixed nationality. It was intended to give Europe a say in matters concerning American atomic power without any new individual European state acquiring atomic power itself. This phantom of the intellect spawned by multi-lateral defence thinking was regarded by de Gaulle with feelings that ranged from benevolent tolerance in the early days to bitter opposition. The negotiations lasted two years, and the longer they went on the more suspicious the General became. In the end President Johnson called off the project in order not to jeopardize NATO, and it was not until then that the French President became more biddable again.

But not for long. For meanwhile the dispute about the European price of grain began to poison the atmosphere between France and the Federal Republic. The problem was this: in view of the Common Market in agriculture the price of grain in the member countries was to be adjusted. It was highest in the Federal Republic, and lowest in France. It was important to adjust prices within the Common Market to the same level because the cost of producing meat, milk, and eggs depended on them. In order to comply with the demand from Brussels, the French aimed at a general lowering of prices while the Bonn government wanted a general raising of prices.

Only someone who realizes the importance of the agricultural groups in the two countries can imagine how serious this dispute was for their governments. It was even more important in Bonn than in Paris, because Erhard knew how vital the farming vote would be in the coming 1965 election. The German farmers were able to prove that the lowering of prices demanded by the French would cut their own income by 1.1 billion DM.

Ludwig Erhard promised them that he would maintain the high price of grain until 1966. De Gaulle, on the other hand, gave an ultimatum: if the EEC did not agree a common price by 15 December 1964, then France would boycott the Community. Thereupon Erhard promised the farmers that he would make good their losses, and this in spite of the fact that he had declared war on all special interest groups and proclaimed that he would never buy anyone off instead of persuading them. Inevitably this seemed like a weakness on Erhard's part, but at least after twelve months of negotiations which had severely strained Franco–German relations he had managed to arrive at a compromise.

But these tiresome problems were as nothing compared to the next catastrophe that was to break over the Chancellor: the Middle East crisis. On 26 October 1964 the *Frankfurter Rundschau* carried an article which revealed the existence of a secret arms agreement between Bonn and Jerusalem. This agreement had been concluded in New York in 1960 between Adenauer and Ben Gurion in response to American suggestions and pressure. It had never been put into writing, and apart from the Defence Ministers (Strauss in 1960, Hassel in 1966) no one knew anything about it. Nor had the Federal Assembly ever been consulted.

President Nasser used the threat that was always used at

that time: unless arms shipments ceased (320 million DM's worth had been promised and 260 DM's worth already delivered), he would recognize the GDR. His threat had credibility, because in the summer of 1964 relations between the GDR and the Third World – and especially Egypt – had become closer in spite of the Hallstein Doctrine. This had for many years been Bonn's much used weapon to prevent all those who had long been ready to accept the idea of two German states from doing so. The Federal Government declared that it would break off diplomatic relations with any state that recognized the German government of the Soviet Zone. Bonn would regard this as an 'unfriendly act'. The débâcle was not Erhard's fault, but he found himself on the horns of a dilemma. Either he must give in to Nasser and alienate Israel, who was in any case displeased because she was still waiting for diplomatic relations to be established between herself and the Federal Republic; or he must let the arms deliveries go on and risk all the Arab countries breaking off diplomatic relations. Today it may be hard to imagine that in the mid-1960s, twenty years after the war, West Germany could still hope to leave a path open for reunification by blocking the recognition of the GDR in the West. But the fact is that until this moment the Hallstein Doctrine had worked almost without fail. A single East African state, Zanzibar, had exchanged ambassadors with East Berlin, in 1964; but when the island united with Tanganyika to become Tanzania, the embassy was downgraded to become a consulate once more.

There was thus great dismay early in 1965 at the news that President Nasser had invited the head of the GDR, Walter Ulbricht, to Egypt. This would be the first visit by the head of the GDR to a country outside the Soviet block. And this visit was shortly to be followed by a Nasser visit to East Berlin. Before any of this could happen, Erhard had declared that arms deliveries to Israel would be stopped and that he regarded Ulbricht's visit as an 'unfriendly act' and would reply to it by stopping economic aid to Egypt. On 24 Feb ruary 1965 Ulbricht arrived in Cairo and signed a number of agreements. Three days later Nasser announced that he would open a consulate-general in East Berlin. Another three days later Erhard announced the end of economic aid to Egypt and the start of diplomatic relations with Israel, an announcement which was implemented on 13 May. Thereupon all the Arab States except for Morocco, Tunis, and Libya broke off diplomatic relations with the Federal Republic.

This was undoubtedly the worst crisis of the Erhard era. But it could not be blamed on any weakness of his; what it showed, on the other hand, was how little clout a divided Germany had abroad, at any rate so long as the Federal Republic clung to its claim to speak for the whole German people. For now it was obvious that the Federal Republic was prone to a special kind of blackmail. And another thing had become obvious too: the Hallstein Doctrine was no longer an effective instrument for keeping other nations on their best behaviour.

This was the reason why, in September 1965, Foreign Secretary Schröder began to modify the Hallstein Doctrine by declaring that diplomatic relations were acceptable with Communist states which had, as it were, 'been born' with diplomatic relations to the GDR. Erhard gave Schröder a free hand, and the Foreign Secretary established German trade missions in most of the East European countries, thereby taking the first step towards full diplomatic relations.

Although there had long been doubts about Erhard's capacity for leadership, it was under his chancellorship that the CDU/CSU won another shining victory in the 1965 elections, when they polled almost 48 per cent of the vote. But only a year later things looked very different: there was a coal crisis, a depression in the steel industry, the administration was threatened by bankruptcy, and anxieties mounted about Germany's economic stability. Erhard was forced to take back many of the promises and bonuses he had liberally announced before the election – a matter of 6 billion DM altogether. Social reforms were stuck fast; vast subsidies were being paid out; and there were disputes not only among the coalition partners: even within his own Party Erhard was unable to achieve unity.

Then the opinion polls showed that the CDU had descended from 48 per cent at the end of 1965, to 38 per cent in June 1966. The head of the Bavarian CDU, Franz Josef Strauss, issued an ultimatum: his Party would demand Erhard's resignation unless he reformed his cabinet before the spring and steered his foreign policy towards France.

But Erhard let things drift. He was so filled with his sense of mission, so certain that he was the man who had put the Federal Republic on the right course, that he was not even prepared to believe that there might have been mistakes. He had once said to Adenauer: 'What do I care about the elections? I know I'm doing the right thing.' But now North Rhine-Westphalia was on the eve of an election, and for the first time Erhard encountered a wave of dissent. He was heckled during the election meetings in the Ruhr, and he riposted: 'Before I leave, you lout, I just want to tell you that but for me and my policy you would have starved to death in your nappies.' When intellectuals such as Günter Grass and Rolf Hochhuth made fun of Erhard's 'new society', supposedly free of 'special interests, and egotisms', he countered, 'That's where the poet ends and the mean little guttersnipe begins'.

On 10 July 1966 elections for the *Land* Assembly took place in the Rhine and Ruhr area. The result was a political landslide. The SPD won almost half the votes, the CDU lost a great deal of ground. Nobody doubted that not Düsseldorf but Bonn was to blame for this. The fault lay with the disunity inside the CDU which was constantly expressed in interviews with the media; and also with Erhard's lack of determination and his failure to take a strong hand. Now knives were sharpened, the battle for the succession began, and the FDP, the coalition partner of the CDU, began to have doubts about the luckless Chancellor.

In mid-August, the then diplomatic correspondent of *Die Welt*, Hans Werner von Finckenstein, visited the Chancellor and had a conversation with him which is very psychologically revealing. Finckenstein began by asking whether Erhard's self-confidence had been undermined by recent events. Erhard replied, 'No, I have not lost confidence in what to do, what must be done. That I know perfectly well. No one can tell me anything about that. The only thing I am no longer so sure about is whether the German people really have the will to freedom I've been trying to instil into them. If I'm disillusioned, then it's only because no one is ever prepared to do anything of their own free will, but only under duress.' To Finckenstein, Erhard's self-confidence seemed strangely unreal in view of the growing faction against him within the Party and also in view of the fact that he alone had been put in the stocks as the sole culprit for all that had gone wrong. 'His self-confidence was not simulated. He almost seemed to glow with the untroubled radiance of a man who is serene because his conscience is clear.'

'Just wait and see if anyone does better than I do,' Erhard said in the same conversation; and also, 'There can be no question of my discussing my departure with anyone.' Two months later, on 27 October 1966, he was told during a Party meeting that four FDP Ministers had resigned. Erhard had never accepted power as a political factor, and he was not going to fight for the power vested in him the previous year by the people, the Party, and its parliamentary fraction. He gave up and returned to the back benches where he could often be seen, though he was towards the end usually silent and withdrawn.

5

Willy Brandt

When a coalition of the SPD–FDP under Willy Brandt and Walter Scheel succeeded the CDU/CSU government in 1969, it was obvious that it would pursue an active policy towards the East. True, the Soviet Union were not any longer prepared to take the initiative with an endless series of fresh offers, for by now the Federal Republic was firmly integrated into NATO; it also had an effective fighting force and atomic weapons were stationed on German soil. Moscow had tried to prevent all these three developments by every possible means.

No one in the West could ever imagine how profound the Russians' anxiety was about the newly created German military force. And yet it could hardly be otherwise in view of their experience between 1914 and 1945. In the Second World War the Russians, fighting alongside the Americans, had taken years to subdue Germany. No wonder the alliance between their powerful former ally and the dreaded German Federal Republic represented the greatest possible threat in their eyes. The Soviet Union was prepared to pay a high price to prevent such a comradeship-in-arms. But the days were now past when the Russians seemed ready to welcome new ideas: those days before the Federal Republic rearmed and joined NATO, after Stalin's death and after the Twentieth Party Congress.

George Kennan, the former Chief of Planning in the State Department, whose Reith Lectures in 1957 had advocated that the two blocs move further apart, often said to me, and said it in his writings too, that he had always doubted whether

it was a wise move to rearm Germany and take her into the
Atlantic Pact. He thought, on the contrary, that American
policy should have encouraged the reunification of Germany.
If the two military blocs had drawn apart with a neutralized,
united Germany between them, he thought, then the tension
would have lessened: It was only when the two parts of
Germany joined opposing military alliances that the situation
became really explosive.

The objection to demilitarizing Central Europe was that if
the rival blocs drew apart, there would be an imbalance
because the Russians would only retreat a few hundred kilometres, whereas the American troops would have to be
shipped back across the ocean. Besides, Adenauer's prime
objective had been continuity. What had made him so trust-
worthy in the eyes of the Occupying Powers was his motto
'No experiments'. For many years it also guaranteed him a
safe majority in German politics. But to him the word continuity meant never altering a decision in the light of new developments. Later on Willy Brandt was to say, 'By recognizing facts we create new facts.' Insights of this kind, however,
were foreign to the old Chancellor. For Adenauer integration
into the West was more important than trying to prevent the
other Germany's integration with the East. Hence there was
no Eastern policy during his Chancellorship, and internal
German policy was confined to a call for free elections. As
the young historian Waldemar Besson wrote before his
premature death: 'For a long time this remained the official
Bonn formula for change in the *status quo*. Adenauer's policy
was much applauded in the Federal Republic, and this ob-
scured the fact that in the prevailing circumstances his policy
was really a refusal to initiate any kind of action, even though
such a refusal was very well founded both morally and politically ... The demand for free elections in the Soviet Zone
of Occupation was out of line with the actual balance of power
in Central Europe: it threatened to deprive the Soviet Union
of her share in the spoils of war without even adumbrating
the question of compensation. This may have seemed im-

pressive to the West, but it was certainly not the foundation for a practicable policy towards the East.'[38]

Germany's European neighbours, and the United States too, recalled the ghost of Rapallo from its grave at every possible opportunity. As late as 1979, a German–American conference in Hamburg was largely dominated by this theme. Anyone who has witnessed the general obsession with Rapallo will understand that in the 1950s Germany's first priority was to create trust. And according to Adenauer trust depended on not exposing oneself to the accusation of conducting a see-saw policy.

Before the new SPD/FDP coalition under Willy Brandt came to power in 1969 with a new Eastern policy in its programme, there was an important intermezzo: the great coalition. A government of the two major parties, the CDU/CSU on the one hand, and the SPD on the other, followed Erhard's defeat in early December 1966. Kurt Georg Kiesinger of the CDU became the new Chancellor with Willy Brandt as Foreign Secretary.

Even in the months before the all-party coalition the subject of Eastern policy had been discussed with unaccustomed vigour throughout the Federal Republic. It was certainly taken into consideration by Foreign Minister Gerhard Schröder in March 1966 when he presented proposals for European disarmament and security to all the governments with whom the Federal Republic entertained diplomatic relations, as well as to all the countries of Eastern Europe and the Arab world. Only the GDR received no proposal because it was not recognized as a state. This so-called peace note, drawn up with the help of Herbert Wehner, was the first document to speak of the necessity of exchanging undertakings of non-aggression, especially with the Soviet Union, Poland, and Czechoslovakia.

During the prelude to the great coalition it was the SPD who took the initiative in the first talks between the two Germanies. The party leadership of the SPD replied to an open letter which the East German SED had addressed to the delegates at a Party conference planned to take place in Dortmund in June 1966. The SED letter suggested to the SPD that they should form a common 'Socialist' front against the bourgeois government. Strangely enough, this proposal for a 'Popular Front' was not thrown into the waste-paper basket but was answered by a counter-proposal: the two parties were to arrange a frank exchange of views at two meetings, one to be held in the GDR and the other in the Federal Republic.

In April it was agreed that Karl Marx Stadt and Hanover should be the venues for these two exchanges. But then the GDR was obviously stricken with fear. It seems that in Eastern Germany, exactly as in the Federal Republic, interest in the theme of the discussions had aroused certain national feelings. This was probably the reason why in June the SED finally withdrew from the exchange of speakers. So the conversation stopped before it had even begun, but nevertheless the ban was broken which for so many years had prevented all contact with the GDR. It was high time: anger in the West was great at the way that Bonn had constantly tried to impede every development; and there was considerable danger that the Federal Republic would remain isolated as the last Cold Warrior in a changed world.

At the Dortmund conference the SPD signalled its readiness to take up diplomatic relations and declared itself ready to abandon the Hallstein Doctrine towards the Eastern European countries. The Party leadership recognized that a peace agreement would demand sacrifices in the matter of border adjustments. This was the first ever hint at such a thing. Both these points reappeared in Federal Chancellor Kiesinger's inaugural declaration: 'With all our might we will try and prevent the alienation of our two peoples during their separation. We want to relax, not to rigidify, to bridge the ditch that separates us, not to deepen it.'

So now the thaw set in: like everyone else the Federal Republic was ready to plunge into the stream of *détente*, to shake off the legal fictions and bureaucratic shackles with which she had increasingly managed to isolate herself. The East, on the other hand, took a sceptical view of the change in politics. The GDR declared that the new line was only 'a trick played by the revanchists of Bonn'; the Soviet Union and Poland remained hostile; only Romania resumed diplomatic relations with Bonn in January 1967. In August 1967 the Federal Republic exchanged trade missions with Prague; and in December she resumed diplomatic relations with Yugoslavia. Moscow's suspicions were shown to be justified by developments in Czechoslovakia: in the climate of *détente* the long pent-up dislike of the old policy asserted itself by toppling the Party's General Secretary Novotny and replacing him with Alexander Dubcek.

1968 was a year of profound unrest and dramatic impetuosity, of great hopes and revolutionary dreams. In Czechoslovakia this first success led to a mood of exultation in which the people took more and more liberties and began to shape their own destiny. Students rioted in France and Berlin; in May 1968 in Paris they were temporarily joined by the workers, and a revolution seemed within the bounds of possibility. De Gaulle was forced to interrupt his state visit to Romania. He returned to Paris where chaos had already broken out, and then flew immediately to visit General Massu at Baden-Baden in order to make sure of the army's loyalty.

In the spring of 1968 the students grew restless even in Poland, and Moscow recognized that it would be difficult to keep the Eastern bloc together in face of the general *détente*. On 21 August, in the midst of all the tumultuous enthusiasm, the Russian tanks rolled into Prague. It was armed intervention: the whole Czech leadership was deposed and the people's hopes crushed underfoot.

Kiesinger's CDU felt that the new Eastern policy had failed, whereas his coalition partners, the SPD, thought that it had been successful in as much as it was the first time the Soviet Union had visibly lost the initiative. In the election campaign of 1969 the CDU/CSU fought a defensive battle with the old arguments, whereas the SPD took the offensive under the banner of an '*Ostpolitik*' or Eastern policy. In March 1969 when Gustav Heinemann, a member of the SPD, was elected to the presidency of the Federal Republic, the FDP had voted with the SPD for the first time. And now, in the general election of 1969, they moved even closer to the SPD because they supported the '*Ostpolitik*'. The result was defeat for the CDU/CSU; the SPD and the FDP together had a narrow majority and formed the Socialist–Liberal coalition. Thus the great coalition had become the missing link between the CDU's four periods in office and the succession to power by the SPD. The SPD was finally released from its role as Opposition party – a role to which it had seemed condemned for eternity.

This at least was my impression – which was shared by hardly any other observer: everyone regarded that period as a sin against the spirit of democracy. An all-party coalition without an effective Opposition, and therefore without sufficient control over the government is, of course, not really to be recommended according to the democratic rules of the game. But in this case it was the all-party coalition that created the premise for the alternation of parties. Apparently the German people needed to see the SPD trotting in double harness with the well-tried horse of the CDU before they could believe that the Social Democrats could give them a perfectly good ride. Perhaps I may quote a balance sheet I drew up at the end of the 1966–9 period:

> For the first time wider sections of the middle classes have discovered that the SPD is capable of governing. Of the three ministers who seem to the public to be the most interesting and effective members of the cabinet – Franz Josef Strauss, Willy Brandt, and Karl Schiller – two belong to the SPD. There has been a profound change in people's attitude to several major concerns: economic and social policy, foreign policy, and legal policy.
>
> To begin with the last: the all-party coalition accomplished more liberal reforms than the five cabinets that preceded it. New laws for State security replaced the old ones which reflected the

spirit of the Cold War; and the paragraphs concerned with moral legislation were thoroughly overhauled.

Erhard regarded any form of economic planning as heresy, whereas Schiller is in favour of overall planning. That is why he introduced medium-term financial planning and the stability laws, why taxation was deliberately adjusted to market fluctuations, why 'concerted action' was invented, and financial, social, and agricultural cabinets were set up. From this angle it became possible at last to tackle the structural crisis in the mining industry. Finally, in May of this year [1969] the reform of the financial constitution enabled us to co-ordinate the planning and financing of three communal tasks, that is, more higher education, regional economic policy, and the structure of agriculture: all these can now be jointly planned and financed by the Federation and the individual *Länder* according to fixed rules. . . .

Under the all-party coalition social policy also underwent a radical change. The underlying principle had always been the assumption that welfare and charity were unfortunately unavoidable: now people are beginning to realize that a welfare policy is essential for reasons of social policy, and that it can also be justified economically as an investment.

Today the Ministry of Labour has the second largest budget (17 billion DM). Social policy is governed by the need to plan for employment, and to adjust to altering circumstances. The all-party coalition's success in doing these things is reflected in the following measures: the vocational training law; the law to promote employment; continuing wage or salary payments; and the equalizing of wages and salaries between Germany's 11 million blue-collar and 5.6 million white-collar workers. All these are largely due to the CDU Minister Katzer: but without the SPD he would never have been able to push his programme through the cabinet – indeed not even to envisage it.

It is astonishing to think of the many things in the field of foreign policy and relations with the GDR which are taken for granted nowadays, but which would have been quite unthinkable in the era of Adenauer and Erhard. For fifteen years no letter from East Berlin had been received or read in Bonn, let alone answered. In 1967 an exchange of letters took place at the highest level between Kiesinger and Stoph: Bonn was offering to negotiate on sixteen concrete topics. . . .

This attempt to encourage a *détente* by official contact with the GDR authorities was not successful: the only reply from them was negative: in 1968 they imposed the necessity of passports and visas. But the Bonn policy was still right in principle.

The Soviet Union also reacted negatively, and for precisely the same reason. It kept balefully noting that the Federal Republic's new Eastern policy was trying to undermine the solidarity of the Socialist camp. Moscow was afraid that Eastern unity would diminish in direct proportion to the spread of *détente*, and therefore formidable barriers were erected to stop the policy from spreading.

So the new flexibility in Germany's Eastern policy unfortunately had no other result than to demonstrate to the world that she was not the culprit responsible for the Cold War – an accusation which it would have been difficult to deny during the Adenauer–Erhard period. And another thing: people's attitude to the East changed. In spite of all the cold water thrown by Moscow, East Berlin, and, in the early days, by Warsaw too, 75 per cent of the population declared itself in favour of continuing Brandt's foreign policy.

So the all-party coalition not only achieved structural changes, it also changed people's consciousness. And this was done in a way which the SPD alone could not have achieved for it could not be said that Brandt's party had a sole lease on the fount of wisdom. Without their partners they would certainly have tried to realize much bolder plans – plans dreamt up in the years of ineffective opposition. But the all-party coalition forced them to recognize the bounds of the possible through practical experience. Now the path is free once more for normal politics with the two major parties governing by turns.[39]

However, this short period was marked by one negative development: the rise and fall of a radical party of the Right, the National Democrats (NPD). From 1964 onwards this party attracted various conservative and extreme Right splinter groups, and after 1966 it suddenly began to be alarmingly successful in various *Land* elections: in 1966 it won 7.9 per cent of the total vote in Hesse and 7.4 per cent in Bavaria; in 1967 7 per cent in Lower Saxony, 8.9 per cent in Bremen, and 9.8 per cent in Baden-Württemberg. The NPD's character may be seen from the fact that it wrote off Auschwitz against Dresden, and deplored 'the spirit of submission'. Its supporters foamed at the mouth at the thought of guitar players, long hair, and people who wanted 'to forget the past'. They were in favour of wholesome family life, national rebirth, and talked a lot about a common destiny: they had no political ideas at all. They were people who had missed the bus, mourners for the past, yesterday's men, but they were neither Nazis nor Fascists – simply reactionaries.

In the Federal Elections of 1969 which marked the end of the all-party coalition, they failed to reach the 5 per cent of the vote necessary to send a delegate to the Federal Assembly; and after 1970 they disappeared from the *Land* Assemblies as bewilderingly swiftly as they had emerged. It is quite possible that this Party was not merely a consequence of the recession, but also an unpleasant side-effect of the all-party coalition: the two major parties jointly governing the country left a gap at the Right end of the spectrum for those who could not bring themselves to share a bench with the 'Sozis'. Besides, the end of the 1960s was the dawn of a new, modern world: these people simply could not or would not keep up.

So, a systematic Eastern policy under the slogan 'security through normalization' began in October 1969 with the new government under the Federal Chancellorship of Willy Brandt. The Russians had already made a few proposals for negotiations, probably in order to wipe out the impression left by the events in Prague. They suggested a European conference on security, and declared themselves ready to discuss Berlin on a quadripartite basis; Gomulka, the first secretary of the Polish United Workers Party, also made proposals for a frontier settlement.

In his inaugural speech of 28 October 1969 Brandt spoke of 'two states in Germany'. He also proposed to the cabinet of the GDR that the two states should hold 'talks at government level and without discrimination in order to prepare the ground for co-operation on a treaty'. Brandt's motto was 'to work side by side until we can work together'. True, he also said (and this remains so today) that the two German states were not 'foreign to one another: their relations can only be of a special kind'. Decoded this means: there is no question of the Federal Republic recognizing the GDR under international law. The Western Powers were advised to 'pursue the talks that had begun with the Soviet Union about relieving and improving the situation in Berlin'. Finally Brandt announced that he intended to suggest a date for the Moscow talks proposed by the Soviet Union; and in answer to a speech by Gomulka he proposed to also start talks with the Polish People's Republic.

This speech left no doubt that the attempt to normalize relations with the East would be rooted in West Germany's adherence to her Western alliances and her membership of the West European Community. The government made an immediate start on the complex new programme which nevertheless had to be divided into many gradual stages. As Brandt himself says: 'My own ideas and proposals had developed over many years. My party put forward its proposals from 1966 onwards when the Kiesinger-Brandt government was being negotiated.'[40]

The basis of all this had to be a treaty with the Russians, because they held the key to the whole undertaking. This in turn meant that treaties with Poland and the GDR needed to be prepared at least in outline; it would therefore be necessary to start exploratory talks with those countries. But it was impossible to recognize the GDR until the Four Powers had decided what to do about Berlin; on the other hand, the Soviet Union would be unlikely to agree to new safeguards for Berlin if the GDR had not first been officially recognized: this too had to be taken into account.

This exceptionally complicated series of diplomatic problems was like having to invent an egg before the existence of the hen: a Chinese puzzle which accounts for the important role played by letters and declarations of intent in the attempt to solve it. In the end the main questions were solved at the right time and in the right order, which proves that the Opposition is unjustified and wide of the mark in their perpetual criticism of the way the SPD/FDP conducted the negotiations throughout those years.

In January 1970, shortly after his inaugural address, Federal Chancellor Brandt sent his Secretary of State Egon Bahr to Moscow for preliminary talks. Bahr had three long series of conversations with Gromyko and with Falin, the then head of the German desk in the Foreign Office. In the first five months he succeeded in reaching certain agreements: the Federal Republic committed herself to recognizing the Oder–Neisse Line as 'inviolable, now and for the future'. The Soviet Union for her part renounced the right of intervention which she claimed to have under the enemy states clause of the UN charter. Furthermore the Federal Republic declared her intent of concluding treaties with Poland, Czechoslovakia, and the GDR which would make 'a unified whole' with the Moscow Treaty. And finally she undertook to work for the inclusion of both German states into the UN. Agreement to the planned treaty was to depend on the satisfactory conclusion of the negotiations on Berlin.

Through an indiscretion, the details of the so-called Bahr document were leaked to the public: angry discussions followed with the CDU/CSU fanning the flames. For twenty-five years the public had been lulled by the illusion that one day everything would somehow right itself if only the old articles of faith were strictly adhered to. Now suddenly everyone realized that there was going to be a second German state after all, and that the areas beyond the Oder-Neisse Line were irrevocably lost. Although this was merely a matter of acknowledging facts and nothing was relinquished that had not been lost long ago, it was still a severe shock for many people.

The cabinet passed the draft treaty, but issued a directive on the formal negotiations that were now to begin. The directive demanded 'that the Four Power negotiations should guarantee the close link between the Federal Republic and West Berlin, as well as unhindered access to the city: without security on these matters no treaty of non-aggression will be practicable'. This meant that unless the outcome of the negotiations over Berlin was satisfactory, the Federal Republic would not ratify her treaty with the Soviet Union.

The Bonn government also drew attention to the inalienable right of self-determination in a letter which the Russians included in the treaty documents: this letter made it clear that to uphold the right of self-determination was not a territorial demand. These then were the foundations of the treaty signed by Willy Brandt in Moscow on 12 August 1970.

It was fifteen years since Konrad Adenauer and Nikita Khrushchev had walked past the guard of honour drawn up at Moscow airport. I still have that picture vividly in my mind and can remember the emotion that crept over me at the time: a strong feeling of unease, even of uncertainty. After all, this was the first official German visit since the war begun by Hitler, a war that had cost this country twenty million lives. Standing there on the tarmac, was I guilty too, even though I had regarded Hitler as an enemy from the very beginning? That is what I asked myself in 1955. Was there any hope that the havoc wreaked by him in the East from Warsaw to Moscow would ever fade from the survivors' memory? Was this a new beginning, or was this occasion merely a line drawn under a chapter ending?

This time my feelings in Moscow were less mixed and less equivocal. For Brandt had come, as he said, 'to turn over a new page of history'. This time I did not feel uneasy but deeply moved, possibly because so many hopes were stirred on both sides. Everyone felt that it was a departure for fresh shores. An experienced correspondent of *Figaro* said to me, with an undertone of reproach and anger in her voice, 'Now I know who your real friends are.' Later many members of the Opposition were to say that the Eastern treaties had been signed in a state of permanent euphoria. That was certainly not true; but this special day was indeed felt by all to be something out of the ordinary. As far as I am concerned, I should not like my friends – or the members of my government – to be totally incapable of human feelings.

After the signing of the Treaty Federal Chancellor Brandt made a speech on television:

> Our national interest does not allow us to stand between East and West. Our country needs to collaborate in harmony with the West, and it needs to come to an understanding with the East. The German people need peace in the full sense of the word, and they need to be at peace with all the peoples of the Soviet Union and of Eastern Europe.... Europe does not end at the Elbe nor at Poland's eastern frontier. Russia is indissolubly bound up in Europe's history, not only as an enemy and a threat, but also as a partner – historically, politically, culturally, and economically. Only if we in Western Europe can contemplate such a partnership, and only if the people of Eastern Europe can also envisage it, only then can we arrive at a balance between our interests.'

For Willy Brandt that day in Moscow must have been one of the great moments of his political life. He is fundamentally a lonely, reserved man. For him, the Socialist youth movement took the place of the family he never had; he was a boy of nineteen when he emigrated in 1933 all on his own from Lübeck. In a television interview with Gaus he once said, 'I do not want to dramatize this business of my difficult childhood – or of my not entirely easy childhood ... I don't want to make it sound more difficult than it was. I was well provided for – that's not the point. But ... well, one was different from other children.'[41]

When in 1930 the SPD had decided to tolerate Brüning's cabinet so as not to drive it into the arms of the extreme Right, many young people regarded this as a betrayal of Socialism. Pragmatism has never been valued by idealist ideologues. Seventeen-year-old Herbert Frahm (Brandt's real name) indignantly joined the Socialist Workers' Party (SAP) which stood to the Left of the SPD. Soon he became its political leader. With his associates he printed and distributed

131

leaflets by night. Immediately after Hitler came to power in 1933 several of his companions were arrested.

Herbert Frahm, who had now gone underground under the name of Willy Brandt, secretly travelled to Dresden to take part in an illegal gathering of his Party. On 31 March he was forced to take flight. A fisherman ferried him across the Baltic by night, from Travemünde to Denmark. He spent the next few years in Norway, learnt fluent Norwegian, and returned to Germany in 1936. In the guise of a Norwegian student he lived in Berlin and worked with the Resistance. In 1937 he spent some time in Spain writing reports for his party colleagues in Paris. Then he returned to Oslo.

Deprived of his German nationality, he was forced to flee once more, when the Germans invaded Norway in April 1940. He disguised himself as a Norwegian soldier and was captured by the Germans somewhere in northern Norway; but they did not recognize him and released him after a few weeks. Then he fled to Sweden. He summed up this period as follows, 'There were Nazis in the German army – and Germans.' Other emigrants were less objective.

During that period he wrote to a Swedish friend: 'If it were true, as some people say, that the whole German people consists of nothing but Nazis, then Hitler would surely not have needed to rule with the help of terror, the Gestapo, and concentration camps.' At the end of 1946 Brandt arrived in the ruins of Berlin as press attaché to the Norwegian military mission. The following year the SPD asked him to take over the party leadership's liaison with the Allied administration in Berlin, and he decided to resume his German nationality. Years of strife followed within the Berlin party. In September 1953 Ernst Reuter died and, after two less prominent successors, Willy Brandt, in 1957, became the ruling Mayor of Berlin.

Whenever I think of Willy Brandt in connection with Berlin an exceptionally impressive scene rises up before me. It was in the autumn of 1956 at the time of the Hungarian rising. Brandt was President of the Chamber of Deputies. The Berlin party had called for an evening demonstration outside the Schöneberg town hall in order to protest against the brutality with which the Soviet armoured vehicles were crushing the revolt in Budapest. About 100,000 people had come together: most of them were probably thinking of their relations and friends who were oppressed in the other half of the city. The mood was indignant, bitter, and angry: at the end of the proclamation a wave of emotion swept over the crowd.

Suddenly there were whistles, cries, and people shouting in chorus, 'To the Brandenburg Gate! Russians out!' Just outside the Brandenburg Gate on the Western side there is a monument to the Russian dead which is always guarded by a Russian guard of honour. The crowd was already moving off, led by young people waving torches. The police were helpless. It was only too easy to imagine what would happen next.

Brandt immediately realized the extent of the danger. From the balcony of the town hall he rushed down into the street, lept into an abandoned police loudspeaker van, and drove towards the Brandenburg Gate. He actually managed to stop the excited crowd. Eventually everyone began to sing the song of the good comrade, and gradually the whole affair subsided. Right at the end Brandt even succeeded in reaching those demonstrators who had already got as far as the sector frontier. He persuaded them to turn back, thus preventing a catastrophe.

Brandt was the ruling Mayor of Berlin at a time when the city was a synonym for freedom in the West, a symbol to which statesmen from all the world came in pilgrimage. He was the head of government when Khrushchev gave his ultimatum, and when the wall was built. Through all those years he gave the people courage and confidence, just as Ernst Reuter had done in his day. In 1958 he dismissed Khrushchev's ultimatum without even consulting the Allies or the government at Bonn. And in 1963, again entirely of his own accord, he sent a telegram to President Kennedy telling him not to allow himself to be blackmailed over Berlin. Willy Brandt often asserted his independence regardless of what people might say and regardless of his own fate. It is said that he was no judge of men and chose the wrong people to work with him: in some cases that cannot be denied. But it is quite unjust to accuse him of being reluctant to take decisions, certainly during the period of his chancellorship.

On the contrary: he moved very fast. As I have already mentioned, the Soviet–German Treaty was signed in Moscow in August 1970. The Polish–German Treaty was signed in Warsaw in December. The negotiations with both countries were extremely difficult, those with Poland particularly on account of the frontier. Bonn did not feel able to draw a definitive Oder–Neisse Line in anticipation of the all-German peace talks which might still take place one day. So Article 1 of the Treaty says that the line laid down in the Potsdam Agreement is 'the Western frontier of the Polish People's Republic'; furthermore the Treaty repeats the clauses about the inviolability of the existing frontiers, and renounces German territorial rights in accordance with the Moscow Treaty. Article 2 contains the undertaking not to resort to force.

In a television appearance in Warsaw on the day the Treaty was signed Federal Chancellor Brandt said, 'The flight from reality creates dangerous illusions. . . . A clear sense of history cannot tolerate demands that can never be fulfilled. Nor can it tolerate those "secret reservations" against which the East Prussian Immanuel Kant warned us in his work *For Perpetual Peace*. We must look towards the future and recognize morality as a political force. We must break the chain of wrongs. If we do this we shall be practising not the politics of resignation, but the politics of reason.'

That too was the occasion when Brandt fell upon his knees – an act which attracted so much comment at the time. A correspondent of the London *Guardian* wrote in an interview with Willy Brandt: 'I asked him about the incident in Warsaw last December when he walked through the former Jewish ghetto to the stone monument erected in remembrance of the 500,000 Jews who were murdered there by the Nazis, and fell upon his knees. What were his thoughts as he knelt? He said, "The act must speak for itself. It wasn't planned. It simply happened. But I am not ashamed of it." '[42]

Time magazine voted him 'man of the year' and wrote: 'Willy Brandt is the first West German statesman who has been ready to accept the full consequences of defeat: the lost territories, the admission of moral responsibility, the acknowledgement of Germany's division. At the same time he invites the Communist countries to extend their relations with the West and thereby to extend the freedom of their own peoples.' Alfred Grosser has written 'At that time the German Chancellor was not only "Man of the Year", but also, as *The Times* said, the only great European statesman. There was an extraordinary degree of unanimity about this; especially in the French press, in spite of the fact that traditionally an "open" Eastern policy on the part of Germany has always worried the French.' Grosser continues:

> Drawing up a balance sheet for the year 1970 the normally unsentimental great Paris weekly *L'Expres* said that Willy Brandt's gesture had been the only sign of humane and moral superiority in any statesman. In Belgium the Minister for Education instructed all the schools to draw attention to Brandt's act. Outside Germany no one spoke of humiliation or revived the idea of collective guilt. It was precisely because Brandt could not explicitly condemn anti-Semitism in the presence of his anti-Semitic hosts in Warsaw that everyone understood what the Chancellor meant; and he repeated it clearly in his speech of 21 March 1971 when he inaugurated 'brotherhood week': 'As I stood in Warsaw at the beginning of December, the weight of recent German history lay upon me, the weight of a criminal racial policy. I did what people do when words fail – and in that way I remembered the millions who were murdered – and remembered them on behalf of my countrymen too. But I also thought that – in spite of Auschwitz – fanaticism and the suppression of human rights are still with us.[43]

Many people both inside and outside the country thought that this was the real birth of a new Germany: when it became possible to elect as her Chancellor in Bonn an emigrant who had once been deprived of his nationality.

When Willy Brandt went to Warsaw he invited Günter Grass, Siegfried Lenz, Henry Nannen and myself to accompany him. I accepted because, after all, for many years I had campaigned for an active policy towards the East. But the closer the time came, the more uncomfortable I began to feel. I had resigned myself to the irrevocable loss of my East Prussian homeland; but suddenly it seemed more than I could bear to watch its cession being signed and sealed, and to drink to the conclusion of the agreement as I should inevitably have to do.

What was I to do? My name was included in the published list. If I withdrew at this point my refusal might be seen as political and might make trouble for Brandt. I kept putting off my decision and only wrote to him at the last moment and with a very bad conscience. So my relief was great when after his return from Warsaw I received a handwritten letter from Willy Brandt in which he said that he could well understand my reluctance. And then he wrote: 'As for blubbing, I was overcome as I sat at my desk preparing the texts for Warsaw. And what I said there – partly for the benefit of people here – I think will have been understood. At least I can hope that you understood it and that you know it was not easy for me.'

It had taken the Federal Republic twenty-three years to bring herself to recognize the Oder–Neisse Line as Poland's western frontier. For millions this was the final farewell to their homeland. To all those I addressed an article headed 'A Cross on Prussia's Grave'. So far as I know, it is the only article from *Die Zeit* ever to have been reprinted in its entirety in *The Times*; I also received a personal letter about it from Dean Acheson, the former American Secretary of State.

The article appeared in *Die Zeit* on 11 November 1970:

> Now the agreement on the Oder–Neisse frontier has finally been negotiated. Soon the representatives of Bonn and Warsaw

will sign it. And sure enough voices will say that the Government has handed over German lands – they will say it in spite of the fact that the cross over Prussia's grave was erected twenty-five years ago. It was Hitler whose brutality and megalomania extinguished seven hundred years of German history. Only until now no one has had the heart to register the death or even to agree that it has taken place.

Home for most people is something beyond reason and description. It is so closely bound up with our lives and our being as we grow up that it sets the standard for the rest of our existence. This is especially true for people from the east. If you were born there, in that vast lonely land of endless forests, blue lakes and broad river valleys, then home probably means more to you than to people who grew up in industrial areas or big cities.

With its open society and freedom for everyone to live their lives as they wish the German Federal Republic is a State worth working for and worth helping to shape. But home? That it cannot be for anyone coming from the east.

My family lived up there in the north-east for hundreds of years – and I only bring this in because my own fate exemplifies the fate of many millions of others. Up there between the Vistula and Lake Peipus what comes first is not loyalty to one's liege-lord, as it does in the West, but one's ties to the land. The rulers kept changing: first there were the Teutonic Knights; then the Poles, Swedes, Danes, Russians and Prussians; they were of secondary importance; what mattered was to cling to the land, to belong to that landscape.

During the Seven Years War, when the whole of east Prussia was occupied by the Russians, the inhabitants acknowledged the rule of the Tsarina Elizabeth. Frederick the Great never forgave the east Prussian Estates for that – and yet it was the most sensible thing they could have done. It was only during the last hundred years that things changed, when the spirit of nationalism began to poison all international relations.

Now that the Germans have been driven from their homeland east of the Oder and Neisse the change of rulers will come to an end. Now the land is Polish. Nearly half the population now living in the former German areas was born there. Like the Czechs in Bohemia, the Poles were ruthless in making a clean sweep. Never before had anyone tried to make sure of the permanent possession of those Eastern lands and provinces by driving eight million people from their homeland. But who can blame the Poles? Never before has a people made to suffer as they were during the period of the Third Reich.

Aided by the SS, Hitler's Governor General Hans Frank tyrannized the Polish population, deported them and sent them to the gas-chambers. He outlined the Nazi aims in a speech: 'No Pole must be allowed to advance beyond the status of a foreman. No Pole will be eligible for higher education in any state institution. I must ask you to obey this clear directive.' And further, 'We have now established who are the leading strata of Polish society: they are to be liquidated. If a second generation appears, they are to be marked down forthwith and eliminated after a suitable interval. . . . There is no need to deport these people into concentration camps within the Reich. That would only give us trouble and involve us in unnecessary correspondence with the relatives: much better to liquidate them on the spot.'

The 'Führer's orders' after the Warsaw rising in the autumn of 1944 were to raze the city to the ground. And the SS never failed in thoroughness or brutality. When they left, only 2000 people remained in the caverns and ruins of a city of millions. No one today can still hope that the lost territories will ever be German again. Anyone who does not agree that this is so must be dreaming of recapturing them by force. That would mean displacing millions of people all over again – and that is something no one can really want. So we must hope that the patriotic groups who consider everyone a traitor who does not take their illusions as reality will now cease their polemics.

All the same it is to be hoped that in future the Poles will spare us their Chauvinism: They talk of 'recaptured territories' and their official publications include statements such as 'Under German rule the Western territories were mostly inhabited by a native Polish population.' The truth is that 98–100 per cent of the population of East Prussia, Pomerania, East Brandenburg, and Lower Silesia was German; Upper Silesia was the only province with a sizeable Polish-speaking minority. East Prussia's Eastern frontier remained unchanged for seven hundred years, and apart from the industrial region of Upper Silesia, the Silesian frontier has not changed since the Treaty of Trentchin in 1335 when Casimir the Great ceded Silesia to Bohemia.

On these questions both sides are in the grip of clichés and far too few people are competent to judge; the history of the East is too complicated and unfamiliar. Moreover many people forget that history is always written by the victors. Who, nowadays in Eastern Europe, ever mentions the secret protocols of the treaties concluded between Hitler and Stalin on 23 August and 28 September 1939? They were the basis on which the Russians synchronized their attack on Poland with Hitler's war: and Moscow appropriated 50 per cent of the Polish State as it was at that time.

The secret agreement did not totally preclude the continued existence of a Polish State; but after the Russian troops had marched into Eastern Poland (and on that occasion too representatives of the ruling strata were deported or killed) Moscow put pressure on the German Ambassador Count Schulenburg to prevent the formation of a Polish rump State.

That has been the desire of Russia's rulers for hundreds of years – ever since the Tsars tried to eliminate Poland as a factor in European politics. Catherine the Great had it in mind when she decided to partition Poland, first in 1772 and then again in 1793: Prussia shared in both partitions, Austria only in the second. At the third partition in 1795 Prussia and Russia co-operated with Austria to wipe out Poland altogether.

And few people remember that at the time of Munich in September 1938 the Poles took Teschen from the Czechs; and that they supported Germany during the Sudetenland crisis so that the government in Berlin was encouraged to make demands which in the long run led to Poland's own collapse.

No one is free from sin. But attempts to try and reckon up between nations are senseless and only reinforce the curse on evil deeds which makes them breed further evil. So do we need a fresh start? Yes, otherwise escalation will never cease. So must we say good-bye to Prussia? No, for the spirit of Prussia must continue its work in these times of material greed – otherwise this state we call Federal Republic will not last.

While the Secretaries of State travelled to Moscow and to Warsaw the Federal Chancellor approached the SED. But they were not prepared to renounce force as long as the GDR had not been recognized under international law. Finally Brandt offered talks without any conditions about the agenda, and Prime Minister Stoph accepted. The talks were to take place at Erfurt in March 1970. The interests of the two sides were diametrically opposed: Brandt was looking for contact in order to minimize the effects of division. Stoph was intent on self-insulation, delimitation, and having as little contact as possible. Willy Brandt's journey from Bonn to Erfurt turned into a triumphal procession from the moment the train crossed into GDR. Presumably this merely increased the fears of Ulbricht and the SED.

No one – including the traveller himself – had dreamed that the appearance of the head of the Bonn government would be so dynamic. People seemed suddenly to be electrified; they were in a state of national excitement such as had never been seen before. The pictures that went round the world were unforgettable and brought tears to the eyes of television viewers in West Germany too. You saw the hotel Erfurter Hof with a densely packed crowd all round it. Suddenly the camera panned to a bay window where Willy Brandt had just appeared. There was an instant's hesitation, a deathly hush, and then the yell of a thousand voices – and it was a yell, not a cry – over the whole square: 'Willy, Willy!' Was it hope? Was it despair? Who knows! At the open window the Chancellor seemed almost startled: his hands rose from the sill in a barely perceptible movement of apprehension – a helpless, beseeching gesture. A few seconds, and he had disappeared: it was all over.

The meeting with Stoph awakened great expectations, but understandably came to nothing. Stoph was prepared to hold a second meeting, but he still insisted that recognition for the GDR must be the first step. The second meeting took place on 21 May at Kassel. Bonn had carefully prepared an agenda of twenty items, but again the talks ended without yielding any result. This time, however, no new date was fixed – perhaps Erfurt had been too great a shock for the Party.

Meanwhile the Four Powers had begun their talks about an agreement on Berlin without direct participation by either the Federal Republic or the GDR. Since 26 March the three Western Powers' ambassadors to Bonn had been sitting with Soviet Ambassador Abrassimov in the former Allied Control Commission building in the American sector of Berlin. Here too the interests of the two German States were diametrically opposed. The Federal Republic wanted guarantees on access to Berlin and on the right of West Berliners to visit the East. Their most important point was that West Berlin should be governed by Bonn and that Bonn should have the right to represent West Berlin and her citizens abroad.

If the Federal Republic were to gain all these points it would mean that the sovereignty of the GDR over the access routes to Berlin would be curtailed. So it was no great surprise that the negotiations were bogged down for several months for there was no agreement even on a starting-point. The Western Powers proceeded on the assumption that the whole city would have Four-Power status; the Soviets, on the other hand, considered the present situation – illegally and unilaterally created by them – to be a valid basis: East Berlin was the capital of the GDR and only West Berlin could be the subject for negotiation. In the end, everyone compromised on this question by never speaking of Berlin as a whole or of West Berlin, but only of 'the territory in question'.

At last, in the autumn of 1971, the moment had come. It was shortly after President Nixon declared his intention of visiting Peking, an announcement which probably was not without its effect on the proceedings: on 3 September the Four Power Agreement was signed by the four Ambassadors.

So now the Soviets had guaranteed civilian transit traffic to Berlin; they had promised to make it easier for West Berliners to visit East Berlin and the GDR; and finally, and this was very important, they confirmed that 'the ties between the Western sectors of Berlin and the German Federal Republic should be maintained and developed'. True, the West had to make concessions too: they had to confirm that, 'As before, these sectors are not part of the Federal Republic and will continue not to be governed by her.' This meant renouncing the sovereignty of the Federal administration in Berlin; but at the same time the continued presence of Federal institutions in the city was confirmed, as well as the rule of Federal law (with the consent of the Allies); and Berlin was to continue to send delegates to the Assembly at Bonn. Moreover, the Soviet Union agreed that permanent residents of West Berlin could be represented abroad by Federal consulates, which meant that they carried Federal passports. The Soviet Union, on the other hand, was permitted to establish a consulate-general in West Berlin which was to be accredited to the three Town Commandants. So there was now a very satisfactory agreement and everything was prepared for its ratification.

In January 1972 negotiations began for a general traffic agreement, which was signed in May. This, incidentally, was the first independent treaty under international law to be signed by the two German states. The last stage in the normalization of their relations was still to come: this was the *Grundvertrag*, the treaty between the two Germanies, which would define their relationship. It was the pre-condition of their joining the UN. Once the GDR was a member of that organization she would be internationally recognized and automatically the Federal Republic would relinquish her claim to be the 'sole representative' of the two Germanies.

The Grundvertrag did not resolve the question of nationality according to the wishes of the GDR because she did not succeed in overcoming the clause in the Federal Republic's constitution which gave every German – including the East Germans – the right to be a citizen of the Federal Republic. The Federal Republic, on the other hand, failed to establish her concept of 'special relations' based on common nationality. The 'question of nationality' was only mentioned in the preamble and only as a matter of principle on which there were differing views.

It must be made clear, though, that in spite of this laboriously negotiated treaty, relations between the two countries were far from normal. Egon Bahr was quite right when he said that whereas previously Bonn had had no relations with the GDR, now at least she had bad ones.

The personality of Willy Brandt was crucial to the credibility of the Federal Republic's new Eastern policy. And the Federal Chancellor also made a great impression in the West. His first public appearance was at a meeting of EEC Heads of State which took place at the Hague on 1 and 2 December 1969. The new impetus for European unity which resulted from this conference was largely, so everyone thought, due to the German Chancellor. At the Hague Brandt said:

> Whether our meeting succeeds or fails will depend on whether we manage to steer the ship of the European Community back into navigable waters. We must not become so involved in our minor problems that we avoid taking those decisions which will make our fellow citizens understand that Europe is more than just a question of market regulations. We must make our young people see that Europe is more than the memory of a dark but glorious past. . . . So I say quite openly: the German Federal Assembly as well as public opinion in my country expect me to return from this conference with concrete agreements about widening the membership of the Community.

He further showed that Germany was no longer willing to follow in the wake of the French in formulating EEC policy. He drew attention to Germany's attitude towards British entry into the Community by demanding that a date of spring 1970 should be set for the start of negotiations.

Three months later Brandt was singularly honoured in London when he was invited to speak before both Houses of Parliament. Moreover, two years later Brandt was the Queen's guest at Windsor – an honour which had apparently been extended to no German politican since the First World War.

Willy Brandt's Eastern policy was undoubtedly his greatest achievement. Until he became Chancellor, the Federal Republic was decried as militarist and revanchiste by the whole Eastern bloc, and especially by Poland. West Germany was invoked as a bogeyman whenever fractious members of the Communist camp needed to be disciplined or the whole group held together. It was the CDU/CSU whose wishful dream provided the pretext for this: in the East their claim to be the sole representatives of the German people and their oratory in favour of reunification were taken as proof of Bonn's aggressive policies. Brandt recognized the reality of the situation, the existence of two German states and the inviolability of their frontiers ('never by force'): this changed the image of the Federal Republic and made a new beginning possible. And Brandt's foreign policy really achieved its aims – in so far as his negotiating partners permitted it.

The same cannot be said of his policy at home. His vision was too bold: he wanted to reform the state and society from the very bottom and creat a 'modern Germany'. His motto was more democracy, especially more social democracy; more justice, more tolerance, more neighbourly love. And he did succeed in stirring up people's moral commitment and their readiness to share responsibility. In March 1971 he told the Federal Assembly:

> Our reforms must be measured against the following aims: a more humane society; equal opportunities in life; more social justice; more freedom for the individual; national and international security; and more participation for the citizen in the work of the community.

Who could fail to agree wholeheartedly with such a programme? But anyone who has ever had any experience of practical politics also knows how many obstacles, adversities and inadequacies lie between such imaginings and their realization; how intractable many people – and almost all circumstances – can be; and what a vast amount of finance is needed, which does not fall from the skies but has to be earned.

Still, the programme was inspiring and expectations rose. People were seized by a completely new feeling about life. A mania for large-scale reforms spread like wildfire, affecting schools, universities, the administration, family legislation. In the autumn of 1970 Jürgen Wischnewski of the SPD declared, 'Every week more than three plans for reform come up for decision in cabinet and in the Assembly'. And two years later the Minister for Labour, Walter Arendt, announced that he had carried out nineteen reforms between 1969 and 1972. These included increasing the pensions of 2.5 million war victims; making hospital care free to nine million people on social relief; providing a contributory medical service for twenty-three million panel patients; and State financial accident insurance for eleven million children from kindergarten to university age. Costs and debts rose proportionally. Only tax reform remained in abeyance.

The defeats of the 1950s had taught Willy Brandt and many others in the SPD that if a party wants to survive a hundred years in an industrial society and in the changed political and social situation of the post-war years, then it must learn to change its thinking. This realization was embodied in the 'Godesberg programme', which had been passed with an overwhelming majority at the Party Conference at Godesberg in November 1959. The leading reformers were Fritz Erler, Carlo Schmid (the Bavarian von Knoeringen) and Willy Brandt. They had prepared the way for the SPD's transformation from a class party to a people's party; and they were determined to jettison 'ideological ballast', as Carlo Schmid called it.

Their programme proclaimed, 'From being a workers' party the Social Democratic Party has become a people's party.' As recently as 1954 the action manifesto had said, 'The workers are the nucleus of the party's members and voters.'

The new orientation meant that the party was now prepared for a pragmatic policy: it therefore had to accept the basic government decisions taken since 1949 because it was now ready to act on the basis of political realities. NATO, the Warsaw Pact, the two German States, and the European

Community could not be made to vanish into thin air. And if the SPD wanted to play a part in the political life of Germany, then they had to proceed from the *status quo* – in other words to accept certain fundamental positions including the establishment of the *Bundeswehr* which they had opposed for so long.

In a great speech to the Federal Assembly on 30 June 1960 the Party Vice-Chairman Herbert Wehner stressed that the government and the Opposition were jointly responsible for foreign policy: 'The Federal Republic is a reliable partner to any agreement she signs, whether the present government or the present Opposition is in charge. This is how we interpret the signs of the times: we must not tear ourselves apart but work together in the framework of a democratic whole, even though we must remain opponents on the practical issues of home policy. Disagreement on internal policies keeps democracy alive. But by deliberately seeking to create enmity between the parties, as some people do, you end by killing democracy – however harmless things may seem at the beginning. Germany is already divided.... She cannot sustain irreconcilable enmity between Christian Democrats and Social Democrats.'

Kurt Schumacher, the first Chairman of the SPD, had still wanted to transform society along socialist lines. But only a year after Godesberg his successor Erich Ollenhauer declared, 'The first objective is to safeguard the existence of the Federal Republic both internally and externally.' Since then SPD policy has aimed not to change society, but to breathe a new spirit into it. That was what was in Willy Brandt's mind in 1969 when he became Chancellor and drew up his programme of reforms.

The new government's campaign for reforms was accompanied and emphasized by the rising of the young. The protest movement had begun several years before and had taken various forms. It was a mixture of neo-Marxist (revolutionary) and radical democratic (reformist) revolt. The rising broke out in Berlin on 2 June 1967 on the occasion of the visit by the Shah of Iran, when a student, Benno Ohnesorg, was shot by the police. The events of 2 June in Berlin served to transform earlier fringe phenomena into a movement which radically changed public consciousness in the FRG: it was known as APO (extra-parliamentary opposition). Red flags appeared at demonstrations everywhere; university notice boards all over the country were covered with wall news-papers as during the Cultural Revolution in China; Herbert Marcuse, a German professor who had emigrated to the USA, emerged from decades of oblivion to be revered as an authority by the anti-authoritarians.

The revolt was against bourgeois everyday life which was felt to be meaningless and unbearable. Award givings and inauguration ceremonies were disrupted and mocked as lu-dicrous charades. 'Smash what smashes you' was the motto. The new world envisaged was infinitely more imaginative than anything Karl Marx had predicted for the period after the death of the state. The movement reached its climax with the Easter risings of 1968 which were triggered off by an attempt on Rudi Dutschke's life. After that the movement began to splinter: the DKP, a party oriented towards the GDR, and the Maoist KPD/ML were founded. Possibly it was the events of Prague which blighted hopes of freeing op-pressed nations and emancipating wage slaves. In any case, the movement did not survive into the next decade.

Success and failure often lie close together. In December 1971 Brandt became the fourth German to be awarded the Nobel Peace Prize at Oslo. In his speech he said:

> It seems to me that at this moment we should also feel close to those who make sacrifices for the sake of their convictions and yet never cease to fight for peace and justice. I think you will understand what I mean when I say that in these last days and weeks I have been gladdened by the thought that many people – and not just in my own country – look upon this occasion as something that concerns them all. And I should like to add just this: how much it means to me that my work was cited as having been done 'in the name of the German people'. So after the

inextinguishable horror of the past it has been granted to me to see the name of my country coupled with the will to peace and harmony.

But no one remains long on the summit. Already in the previous year three FDP delegates had gone over to the CDU/CSU, so that the Brandt/Scheel government's majority was cut to six. Now, after the first reading of the Eastern peace treaties, which practically gave away the eastern provinces to Poland, in February 1972, Hupka, the delegate representing the refugees, left the SPD in anger and joined the CDU Parliamentary Party. The majority was now down to five. Two months later another FDP delegate, the farmer Wilhelm Helms, decided to leave his Party. All sorts of rumours began to spread about the motives and reasons for these changes, until ultimately only two FDP members remained, and they were far from certain.

The CDU/CSU did brilliantly in the Württemberg-Baden *Land* elections. They then decided to take a risk and do what had never been done before in the Federal Assembly: they tabled a motion of no confidence in the Federal Chancellor, and suggested that the leader of the CDU/CSU Parliamentary Party, Rainer Barzel, be elected in his stead.

Three days later, on 27 April 1972, the motion was put to the vote. The Foreign Minister Walter Scheel made a moving and statesman-like speech: 'Today,' he said, 'every single representative is called upon to make a decision which will have far-reaching political consequences. We are faced with an attempt to alter the political majority without allowing the electorate to participate. Whether or not this is technically legitimate, it is an act which strikes at the nerve of our democracy. If it becomes the rule for parliamentary majorities to be altered by changing the party in power without consulting the electorate, then parliamentary democracy will lose its credibility.'

Addressing the CDU/CSU members he continued:

Come what may, this government has left a deep mark on the

post-war history of our people. It has justified itself historically if only because with its bare majority it did what other governments with large majorities either could or would not do: it led our people across the threshold of their taboos and away from their illusions; it confronted them with hard truths about their position: and by doing that it safeguarded what was left of value after two defeats in two world wars. We cleared up the rubble and bloodied our fingers doing it. You did not help us in this hard political slog, ladies and gentlemen. You mocked us and vilified us, and now you want to enjoy the fruits of our labours. And even if you succeed, you will not diminish our pride in what we achieved under the most difficult conditions.

All I want to do is to remind every single delegate of the grave responsibility resting on his shoulders. Give our people one more year of internal peace, and then let us all together face the decision of the voters. Do not make our country and yourselves unhappy by trying to establish a government at the wrong time and by the wrong means – a government that would have to rely on political renegades for its basis, and whose birth would be blemished by broken oaths.

Barzel was two votes short of an absolute majority. The ballot was secret, but everyone was convinced that the missing votes were from his own party. Very soon a rumour spread that the CDU delegate Julius Steiner had abstained and had received 50,000 DM from the treasurer of the SPD for doing so, but even a parliamentary committee of investigation was unable to throw light on this murky affair.

On 28 April, the vote on the budget of the chancellory took place. The result was a draw with 247 votes for each side. There was a call for new elections. The date for the ratification of the Eastern Treaties, 17 May, loomed on the horizon: if the election was brought forward, the whole complicated parliamentary process would have to be repeated. Great efforts were made to get the treaties through earlier. The Moscow Treaty was passed by 248 votes to 10 with 238 abstentions, while the Warsaw Treaty went through with 248 against 17 with 230 abstentions.

The members of the Opposition could not agree amongst

themselves. They fought for a decision until the very last minute. On the eve of the vote the leader of the Opposition, Rainer Barzel, and several other delegates had intended to vote in favour of the treaties; but the next morning they found themselves under heavy pressure from an anti-treaty group led by Strauss, the Chairman of the CSU, and Gerhard Schröder, the deputy Chairman of the CDU. The Parliamentary Party finally agreed on a magic formula: they would abstain: not a very impressive achievement from the strongest party in the Assembly on such an important issue.

After the elections in November 1972, the SPD for the first time emerged as the strongest party in the Federal Assembly. Barzel's attempt to bring down the Chancellor had outraged many voters, and they reacted by voting for Brandt. Moreover, Brandt's Eastern policy had converted many people into committed Party members because they appreciated his efforts in favour of peaceful co-existence. Günter Grass started a Social-Democratic election campaign, and many writers, artists, and journalists actively participated. Never had relations between those in power and the intellectuals been so easy or so naturally amicable and positive as under Willy Brandt – a man who was always more interested in ethical initiatives than in power politics. He led not by authority but by persuasion, with lengthy discussions in which he showed infinite patience: his tendency to philosophize on politics, to favour broad designs and inspiring visions was what attracted the intellectuals to him.

But it was perhaps those very qualities that eventually became his undoing. In the everyday business of government and administration his style gradually became a liability. The words 'weak leadership' were more and more frequently heard, and there were complaints about decisions not being taken. In her book Carola Stern cites an example of such complaints:

In September 1972, at the end of his first period in office, editors from *Der Spiegel* asked Brandt how the impression of indecisiveness could have arisen during the preceding twelve months: 'Did you ride your cabinet on too loose a rein?' And Brandt replied: 'Yes, yes, you can call it that. I have had to learn from bitter experience during the past year, and from bitter disappointments too ... how to handle certain forms of collaboration. But in the basic matter of relationships with others, Willy Brandt is now too old to be remodelled.' The Chancellorship crisis of 1973–4 did not fall from a clear sky.[44]

But for the time being successful ventures occupied the foreground: President Brezhnev's visit in May 1973 was a success; the first appearance by a German head of government before the UN made a very favourable impression. But then the wind changed. The Chancellor had to cut short his visit to New York because he and his colleagues were worried by harsh criticism from Herbert Wehner, the grand old man of the SPD.

During a visit to the Soviet Union Wehner, the Chairman of the SPD parliamentary group, had described the Chancellor as 'flabby' and 'remote' – and he had chosen to do this in Moscow, of all places, and in front of the accompanying journalists. He also said that Brandt's demands in regard to the Eastern policy were excessive. Once one of the most important members of the party leadership had been so critical, others quietly assumed the right to criticize as well. At the end of the year Brandt's popularity had fallen considerably in relation to the previous year. And as usual in such cases, the press, who previously had praised him to the skies, now grew particularly merciless.

In the spring of 1974 the new wage-level agreements came into force. The Chancellor had repeatedly warned against two-digit increases. But the unions behaved as though warnings from the head of government were no concern of theirs. They settled for 11 per cent, thereby emphasizing Brandt's helplessness. His Party suffered heavy losses in different elections of the *Länder* and the situation grew increasingly precarious. But it was the Guillaume affair that was finally decisive.

Günter Guillaume had 'fled' from the GDR in 1956 – in fact, he had been planted as an agent. He succeeded in working his way up from a Party office in the provinces to the Chancellor's Office where he was in charge of Party and union affairs. In the summer of 1973 Brandt had taken him to be his assistant while he was on holiday in Norway, and Guillaume had had access to highly secret documents. This happened in spite of the fact that there had been suspicions about Guillaume back in the spring of 1973; the Chancellor however had been only partially informed about them. A whole year then passed before there was enough evidence to arrest Guillaume. On top of this, rumours began to circulate about the Chancellor's private life.

It seems that Willy Brandt made his final decision of whether to stay or go dependent on a conversation with Wehner – perhaps because Wehner had been his sharpest critic. According to Brandt, Wehner assured him that he would stick by him whatever he decided. But it seems that Willy Brandt read something else between the lines of Wehner's declaration. His letter of resignation is dated 6 May. That same evening he left the Chancellor's Office.

But he did not leave the stage. He was ready to continue serving the country and the Party as Chairman of the SPD. And there he became indispensable to the Party and to the government. The feeling of ideological undernourishment which befalls many, above all the young, faced with Schmidt's pragmatism, is somewhat compensated by Brandt's presence.

Brandt is today still capable of registering and on occasion articulating what motivates people. His loyalty is in the first place human and not party-political; he also stands up for those who, because they see problems in a different light to Bonn, are a nuisance to the governing. When in May 1981 the chairman of the Baden-Württemberg SPD, Eppler, was labelled yet again as the arch adversary of the government, Willy Brandt said, 'As long as I am chairman of the SPD I would like to see to it that people like Erhard Eppler continue to take an active part in our work and that they can ascertain that it is worth while'.

Adenauer and Schmidt have probably accomplished more for the Federal Republic than Willy Brandt. But when the future citizens of this country remember perhaps merely their names, history will still tell of Brandt's genuflexion in Warsaw. For that is the stuff from which myths and legends always originate. But one has to realize that this only applies to those who are truly genuine – advertising and public-relations agencies could not produce this effect.

6

Helmut Schmidt

No one doubted for a moment whom Brandt's successor would be. It had to be Helmut Schmidt. However, before Brandt's departure, immediately after the Guillaume affair became known, the leading Social Democrats met at Münstereifel in order to decide what should be done. Helmut Schmidt spoke very forcefully against Brandt's going, although he had been the one who had kept complaining about the Chancellor's indecision. He argued that it was unthinkable for a German Federal Chancellor to be brought down by a Soviet agent. But on the following day it was clear that Willy Brandt was not to be swayed, and so on 16 May 1974 Helmut Schmidt was elected Chancellor with 267 votes out of 492.

Schmidt immediately called a meeting of the Parliamentary Party, even before the President had handed him his seal of office. He gave full rein to his displeasure. The Party itself, he said, was responsible for losing millions of votes. They had made gigantic promises without any sense of what was feasible, and they had lost touch with the electorate. At the Hamburg *Land* election two months previously the SPD vote had dropped from 55.3 per cent in 1970 to 44.9 per cent. And a recent poll had revealed that in the Republic as a whole the Party's popularity had sunk below 30 per cent.

Schmidt was determined to lose no time. He formed his government with record speed. Three days after his nomination the new cabinet was ready. The inaugural declaration followed a week later. It was short, and concentrated. His guide-lines for the new government were: 'At a time of increasing worldwide problems we shall concentrate soberly and realistically on essentials – on what is necessary at this time; everything else must be set aside.' Most people guessed what this meant: the end to all reforms.

In any case people had grown somewhat tired of reforms. They realized that increased spending does not automatically lead to improved quality – as in education, for instance, where in a few years the budget had risen from 16 billion to 50 billion DM. Nor could they ignore the fact that more spending did not solve all problems; in fact it created new ones, such as a *numerus clausus* for universities, a surplus of school teachers, and absurd admission procedures. Many people were disappointed because their expectations of greater democracy and greater emancipation had not been fulfilled. In many cases nothing had happened except an increase in bureaucracy. The amount of freedom had not increased, only the opportunity for misusing it, because determined minorities had profited from the chance to acquire positions of power.

In spite of all this, many young people and Leftists were not happy with the new style or the new tone. They complained of too much pragmatism and too little idealism. They were not ready to bid farewell to the vision of a great new beginning that would change everything. They were not interested in small steps, careful experiments, pragmatic changes: they wanted a new society, an alternative way of life. For the time being these hostile feelings were still held in check and concealed by Helmut Schmidt's great success and by the exceptional regard he enjoyed throughout the world. But this was soon to change. In February 1975 Herbert Kremp, a conservative journalist, wrote as follows:

> Disappointment came swiftly and vehemently, and it is just as difficult to explain as the early bonus of trust that immediately preceded it. But Schmidt's sense of irrational processes in politics is not particularly developed. He strives to keep 'facts' and 'philosophy' in separate compartments, and denies their mutual interdependence.

This brings us to one of the most important reasons for the

Federal Chancellor's failures, both then and later. He does not merely proclaim pragmatism, he positively embodies it: and that makes him the enemy of the idealogues and Utopians who are to be found not only in the ranks of the Social Democratic Party, but also among the most powerful forces in the intellectual life of the Republic. Here we have out and out enmity. Böll *has* to be against Schmidt. But that is no laughing matter. For an SPD Chancellor is morally obliged to be of the Left: and he needs the assistance of the intellectual Mafia in the media and in the academic professions for his public relations and propaganda if he is to continue to represent his failures as successes.

This was the secret of Willy Brandt whom the intellectual priesthood had chosen to be their Sarastro. He was their type – the remorseful German, with his revulsion from power. Schelsky defines this priesthood as the group that sets the tone, determines the ethos, and gives out the prizes in the world of the media, the writers' unions, and the reconstituted educational institutions. What they want is not so much a share in decision-making as to make all the decisions themselves. They want to determine how people are to feel, think, and judge. By association Brandt himself had become a member of this caste, and now he rolled out the red carpet for its ascent to the throne.

Schmidt, on the other hand, disputes the priesthood's right to rule. Not only just at the present moment, but in general, because he is opposed to them by nature. He is 'the other', the ideologically flexible type. The priesthood therefore calls him a 'manager'. It is their word and intended as an insult, because a 'doer' cannot be a 'seer'. The future does not belong to him. It is enemy territory to him. He will perish there.[45]

In 1974 there were also elections for the Federal Presidency. On 1 July Walter Scheel succeeded Gustav Heinemann. But this time it was really just a changing of the guard and not a change of power as it had been in 1969 when Heinemann, a Social Democrat, became number one in the state.

The new Federal Chancellor swept through the country like a whirlwind. At the SPD Party Conference in Hamburg he attacked his party comrades:

What do you suppose the workers are interested in at the Witten steel refinery? Or the people on short time at vw or nsu or in Wolfsburg or Emden? What do you suppose the employees of the Hamburg savings bank or of Iduna care about? Or the people on Howaldt? Debates about theory are necessary – yes: one needs fundamental principles. And I am conceited enough to think that I have contributed a good deal to them in the course of my life: several books, a series of scholarly essays, and the first draft of a long-term programme. But there is a difference between discussing things in one's study among comrades and turning an intellectual wrestling match into the basis for a party of public consensus.

Kindly go to the conferences of Union delegates, go to the Union officials' meetings, go to the meetings of the worker members of our Party, and then you will understand what the workers are really concerned with. And don't try and get by with theoretical declarations of loyalty to their interests.

During this conference he also declared that: 'World economics are in a state of crisis which you refuse to understand. You only think about the crisis in your own minds instead of the economic conditions that have to be faced.' This sentence caused much bitterness and protest, especially among the young Left. Schmidt was accused of strengthening anti-intellectual prejudice, of destroying the basis of the Party, of sacrificing reform. The upshot was that he was labelled a mere manager.

Schmidt does not care. He does not think much of people who want to change the system by planning in thin air, who have never had to put their ideas into practice, who have never needed to win a consensus majority – which is to him the most important part of democracy. Besides, everyone has to take it from him. Very soon he was equally hard on the employers. At a meeting of the Federal Union of Employers he growled, 'Why don't you stop pretending that it is the government that sets wage levels in Germany?' And he had a bash at the pessimism which seemed *de rigueur* among employers and told them to stop behaving as though they were an alternative party. On the other hand he kept repeating to the labour unions that profits must rise at a faster rate than wages, in order to attract more investment and create more jobs.

The exceptional efficiency of the Schmidt style of government became apparent very soon. There was a daily morning session, attended only by the most important members of the government, in which the current situation was discussed. Once a week there was a coalition lunch: there always had to be an agenda, at least in outline, to prevent time being wasted. Cabinet business was now conducted, with clarity, precision and briskness. Very often it is the Chancellor himself who puts the most important question, which has often been forgotten by the rest: 'Can we get it through the Assembly?' Here his experience as leader of the Parliamentary Party stands him in very good stead. Afterwards he himself summarizes the outcome of the cabinet meeting for the minutes, and usually the decisions taken include the line of action to be followed. After that the Head of the Chancellor's Office goes into action and gives instructions for the decisions to be implemented.

Under the new head of government the Chancellor's Office functions like a secretariat-general: the wheels run smoothly, silently, and with precision. By silently I mean that unlike former years there are rarely leaks from cabinet meetings, for Schmidt demands the utmost discretion. But on the other hand he is extremely frank with his colleagues and demonstrates his great trust in them.

Brandt's aim was to integrate different interests and points of view to obtain a consensus, which was naturally very time-consuming. Schmidt's aim is to get decisions. Under his leadership discussions are conducted very economically and always aimed at reaching a conclusion. As soon as there is a majority, he passes on to the next point. True, Schmidt enjoys discussion; he is a good listener and thorough in his questioning: but he will never let a debate get out of hand. There is no time for philosophizing. 'Discussions must lead to results, results to decisions, and decisions to action.' That is his motto.

It is easy to see that his breathless, strenuous days only leave time for absolute essentials. When an interviewer asked him whether an industrial society with such complex problems could be governed as a parliamentary democracy at all, he replied: 'Certainly it can. But in the age of television, of mass circulation newspapers, and of rapidly spreading public moods no one should imagine that it is an easy business. There is no doubt that you need more than half your time and energy – perhaps two-thirds – to obtain the agreement of committees and commissions, of the Federal Assembly and of public opinion for decisions which you yourself have long since taken; and that is so not only in Germany.'

The need to order, to analyse, to act, and to get results is always uppermost in Schmidt's mind. Many people therefore think of him only as an administrator and technocrat, and fail to notice that the passion to serve the *res publica* of which Max Weber spoke is also part of his make-up. This passion is rooted in a more profound base than the busy-ness of the manager. Political leadership without moral principles, without mental discipline is unthinkable to Schmidt. 'Politics without a conscience tend towards crime', he says. 'As I see it, politics is pragmatic action for the sake of moral ends.'

Helmut Schmidt is no glib manager; he is a reflective man, occasionally given to melancholy, inclined to caution, always circumspect. But when something has to be done, when it is a matter of making rapid decisions with a cool head and then taking energetic action, then there is no one to equal him. That is how it was during the catastrophic floods in Hamburg in 1962 when three hundred people were drowned. It was Schmidt who kept control of the whole affair. He was Senator for Home Affairs and not really responsible, but he seized command of the administration, the rescue services, and the army. And again during the series of terrorist coups in 1977, especially at the height of the Mogadishu crisis, he was manifestly in charge.

Even before the end of 1974 the economic barometer predicted a new low. The oil crisis of the autumn of 1973 began
to show up, even though for the moment the Federal Republic was still in a better position than most other countries.
She still had the hardest currency, the largest currency
reserves, the largest export surplus, and the lowest price
increases.

In October 1974 the magazine *Newsweek* drew its readers'
attention to these facts in an article which said:

> Schmidt has had to tread on a large number of corns to gain his
> objectives. There were times when he treated his cabinet like a
> pack of naughty children. At the very first meeting he asked his
> Ministers of Finance and Economics to sit directly opposite him
> 'so that I can hear you better'. Recently he slapped a long list of
> 253 urgent projects down on the table with the remark that he
> expected all of them to be fulfilled by the next election, that is
> within 750 days. Some of his ministers heard him shout 'NO!'
> and bang the table when they put up suggestions for expenditure
> with which he disagreed.

In the same month the *Daily Telegraph* was full of admiration: 'This is the first time since the war that it has been
possible to describe this country other than as an economic
giant who is also a political dwarf. Under Helmut Schmidt
the Federal government has thrown off its historical hang-
ups and begun to exercise an influence in world politics
commensurate with its economic strength. When Helmut
Schmidt, the Chancellor, and Hans Apel, his harsh Finance
Minister, call for other countries to pull up their anti-infla-
tionary socks and stop treating the Federal Republic as a milk
cow, then numbers of outsiders are shocked. And so are many
German diplomats.'

But then the situation in the Federal Republic rapidly
began to deteriorate. In 1975 the deficit in the budget had
almost doubled. A new loan of 22.8 billion DM had been
foreseen; in fact it came to 40 billion. People began to realize
that the efficiency of the Welfare State had been exaggerated.

The criticism was that the State had been increasingly turned into a welfare institution, which naturally meant that it had to appropriate an ever-increasing share of the welfare product. In a democracy whose chief aim was to please, the demand for spending always exceeded the income, even if this rose from year to year. For years more was asked of the economy than it could produce. And this has not only been the case just recently; experts think that the process began in the fifties. So it became necessary to ask what the limits of the welfare state were. But no one knew the answer – or rather, no one dared to give one.

Unemployment went on increasing while production slowed down and prices rose. Even the convenient old prescription for obtaining full employment by means of a bit of inflation no longer seemed to work. This state of affairs applies more or less to the whole western world, because by now the worldwide nature of the recession has become apparent. Indubitably this was partly because the fixed tariff for the international conversion of currency had been wrongly set – a mistake which in fact became apparent at the turn of the sixties.

For years the Mark had been overvalued and there had been an enormous export surplus with corresponding deficits among Germany's partners. The surplus in turn was wrongly interpreted as a signal for expansion and led to wrongly conceived investment, in the motor industry, for instance, which began to expand at a time when it would probably have been better to have stabilized it. Gradually the general recession escalated until there was a worldwide economic crisis. Not until 1976 was there a slow and temporary upward swing; but the faulty infra-structure remained.

The set-backs were not confined to the economic field. The international political situation also changed. In America President Nixon's forced resignation had considerably increased the influence of the Senate. The people's representatives were determined never again to give the incumbent of the White House a free hand to do as he pleased: they were going to defend their own prerogative. Ever since Roosevelt Presidents had presented Congress with more and more *faits accomplis* and had tended to outmanœuvre the representatives. Now the latter were determined to resume the right of co-determination which was theirs by virtue of the constitution. That was why Congress insisted that in return for credits and preferential terms the Russians must permit a number of Jews to leave the USSR. This 'Jackson amendment' brought in by Senator Jackson resulted in the indignant Russians cancelling the trade agreement that had already been concluded: that was the beginning of the end of *détente*.

This was bound to have its effect on the Federal Republic in the foreseeable future. For if *détente* is not working between the great Powers, the smaller ones are deprived of their room for manœuvre as well. Bonn had got its fingers burnt as early as July 1974 when the new government decided to situate a planned Federal Office for Ecology institute in Berlin. The moment this was announced the GDR broke off negotiations on all other matters. It became obvious how flexibly agreements with the East can be interpreted. The opinion in Bonn was that the passage in the Treaty between the two German states which spoke of 'maintaining and developing the ties between West Berlin and the Federal Republic' meant that the decision about the institute was perfectly in order; whereas the GDR described it as an illegal attempt on the part of the Federal Republic to extend the Bonn rule to Berlin.

Again there were hold-ups on the roads to Berlin, and again, as in the past, the three Western Powers made a *démarche* and reminded the Soviet Union that she was responsible for the free flow of traffic to Berlin. There were protests on both sides. In the end both sides calmed down. The ecological institute remains in Berlin and does its work there, but the GDR has shown – and Bonn has understood – that more than the maintenance of the *status quo* is not to be expected.

In February 1975 the Opposition leader Peter Lorenz, chairman of the CDU, was kidnapped by five terrorists in Berlin. The citizens of the Federal Republic had already had a number of experiences with the Baader–Meinhof gang, and a few months previously the President of the Berlin Court of Appeal, Günter von Drenkmann, had been shot dead as he opened his front door in answer to the bell. Nevertheless, this new act of violence had a more disturbing effect than the previous ones, perhaps because the whole affair was so long-drawn out. For a whole week the terrorists had the State in their power while a crisis committee consisting of the Chancellor, the Party leaders, the heads of the *Länder* governments and senior officers of the security forces met in the Chancellor's Office in Bonn. In the end the terrorists' demands were met: they were given radio and TV signals, and finally an aircraft was put at their disposal to fly them to Aden.

I was at the Chancellor's residence on the last evening, just as permission to release the terrorists was given. I witnessed Helmut Schmidt's anger and depression. If he had had his way the terrorists would not have been given their freedom. Two months later, in April 1975, another incident occurred and German diplomats in the Stockholm Embassy were taken hostage. The Chancellor immediately put on the brakes. The demand to release twenty-six members of the Baader–Meinhof gang from prison simply could not be met, even though the terrorists threatened to shoot a hostage every hour, and two attachés in fact lost their lives.

On this occasion Schmidt and the Opposition leader Kohl were in complete agreement on taking a firm stand. In the case of Lorenz, both the crisis staff and the country as a whole had been equally divided on the two possibilities: 'Yes, let the terrorists go free in order not to endanger Lorenz's life'; or, 'No, on no account – it will only lead to further criminal acts.' A nationwide poll taken afterwards showed 31 per cent in favour of a firm stand, and 56 per cent in favour of giving in.

For a whole week there was no other topic of conversation,

at home, at work, or in bars and restaurants. In the editorial offices of *Die Zeit* opinion was divided as everywhere else. My commentary in the issue of 7 March 1975 was in favour of a firm stand. As it was the first case of a dilemma which later on was to torment us repeatedly, I reprint it here:

And where were all those people who are always so fond of talking about a sense of duty towards the State, about lack of responsibility towards the community as a whole? What did the CDU hard-liners Jaeger and Dregger say when people were discussing whether the peremptory commands of the blackmailers should be fulfilled or not? They were silent. They waited until the consensus of all the parties and authorities had been ascertained, until the decision had been taken and acted upon; then Jaeger proclaimed his opinion: 'If the CDU had been in power in Berlin, then the terrorists would have long since been captured.' And Dregger took the line of demanding the restoration of the death penalty in certain cases.

It must be admitted that taking that decision was like walking a tight-rope between different ethical motivations: to establish priorities was a nightmare. It is quite understandable that there were no volunteers rushing to take part. It was – everyone felt this – one of those historical decisions which become foundation stones in the life of a nation, because they are both symbol and substance; because they are the material from which the carpet of history is woven.

For it is not just a matter of humanity: 'a human life must be saved whatever the cost'; nor of mere pragmatism: 'on no account must precedents be set or imitators encouraged'. The rule of law is at stake and therefore the very basis of society.

Most people say that it is the business of the State to protect the life of the individual. But what if more and more hostages are taken until, though a dozen individual lives may be spared, life for everyone becomes a farce? It is impossible to shake off the suspicion that the exclusive emphasis on this one priority implies the denial of all other loyalties. And what is the purpose of the State? Does it really exist for the individual? Is it not rather the duty of the State to guarantee the existence and the function of society? Or are the State and society really identical?

No, the State and society are not the same thing. The Dutch

word for society is significant: it is *samenleving*. Society is living together: but the State is the political organization by which society gives itself authorities, laws, and institutions. As the State is rooted in the constitution it must be constant, for the constitution can only be changed if there is a two-thirds majority. But society is the sum of individual citizens whose standards, views, and habits are constantly changing. In other words, the architects of the constitution built their house to last: but the people who live and rule in it change.

Society is not just the sum of individuals. It is something qualitatively different, which on occasion may demand sacrifices. It is difficult to speak of 'the last things' of politics, because in this sphere, too, fashions change, and so do opinions as to what is or is not progressive. And also because there are clichés which are pasted all over certain topics so that they lose all their nuances: law and order is a concept of this sort.

Perhaps it is easier to choose an example from literature – which, after all, is sometimes only a translation of politics. The Elector in Kleist's *Der Prinz von Homburg* is certainly not a simple law and order figure. He is chained to his authority as Prometheus is chained to his rock. He knows that this weakens him because it deprives him of all freedom of action, but he also knows the strength that the ethos of the law gives him which he must never put at risk. That is why the Prince is sacrificed to the ethos – to the point of absurdity; only his own realization that it must be so can save him, together with the mercy of his uncle the Elector.

Every system of society has its own specific credo. The most important values in a democratic constitutional State are human life and the independence of its own institutions and organs, for they guarantee maximum freedom. But there is no democratic model which, once established, will serve unaltered for all time.

Taking hostages for the purpose of forcing certain political decisions is a crime that endangers the whole modern world. Society's reaction is apparent in the growing demand for revenge and atonement. In the long run it will take a very skilful leadership to keep society's reaction in bounds. The task will not have been made easier by Bonn's decision to release from prison five lawfully condemned criminals in response to blackmailing demands.

Three or five young terrorists who could shake the very foundations of the State – we shall only gradually learn what that can mean.

As we have seen, opinion was divided as to what should be done in the Lorenz case. On the whole the CDU was more in favour of giving in. Strauss's own views had been given on another occasion, after Drenkmann's murder but before the Lorenz case. With the 1976 elections in view he addressed a meeting of CSU functionaries behind closed doors at Sonthofen. What he said was then published in *Der Spiegel*. At that time Strauss dealt with all these questions as follows:

> To say, here and now, that all democrats in the SPD/FDP and CDU/CSU must stand together in this situation to save the constitution – that is rubbish. What we should say is that the SPD and the FDP are abandoning the State to criminals and political gangsters. And there is no difference between criminals and political gangsters. They are all of them law breakers. And if *we* take over we will clean up so that for the rest of the century not one of these bandits will ever dare to open his mouth in Germany. Even if we can't quite manage to keep that promise, that is the impression we must give.

In the autumn of 1975 there was a mammoth meeting in Helsinki, the Conference for European Security and Co-operation. Everyone had turned up, even if they did so without enthusiasm: there were presidents, heads of government, and party leaders from thirty-five countries: Communists, capitalists, and representatives of the Third World. Both President Brezhnev and President Ford were there, as were the heads of the two German governments. Even Archbishop Makarios and his mortal enemy, the Turkish Prime Minister Demirel, attended. They all promised to treat one another according to 'the concepts of humanism' and never again to cross their neighbours' frontiers by force. None of these undertakings, of course, were binding agreements: they were merely declarations of intent.

No one expected that any problems whatsoever would be

solved at a meeting of representatives of so many different ways of thinking for such problems naturally arise from *real* difficulties. But for the Europeans there was one major point of satisfaction: during the whole two and a half year period of preparation the Common Market representatives had spoken with one voice. Their idea was that in order to achieve greater security within Europe it is not enough to maintain the *status quo*; on the contrary, there must be opportunities for changing the existing situation by peaceful means. And furthermore: *détente* must benefit not just the nations, but every individual.

It was their first meeting for the two German leaders Helmut Schmidt and Erich Honecker. Both felt that they had grown closer to one another, even though Schmidt had not failed to vent his annoyance over the Guillaume affair. On the other hand he let it be known that as far as he was concerned he had not thought it a particularly brilliant idea to set up the Federal Office for Ecology in West Berlin. Many people thought that the German Chancellor's speech in the plenary session was the clearest and frankest of all. He had quite plainly called for the barriers to be torn down between different people and different points of view; for the right to alter frontiers by peaceful means; and for the reunification of Germany. Brezhnev applauded long and ostentatiously: perhaps he had expected worse.

Schmidt found it much harder to talk to the Polish Premier Gierek, who had made a pointedly hostile speech. Schmidt, accompanied by Foreign Secretary Genscher, went to call on him at his residence; they were firmly determined to reach an agreement of some sort. The conversation went on for eight hours. The sun had begun to rise when they finally agreed on the number of Germans who were allowed to leave Poland and on the sums to be paid over.

An important change took place in the second half of the seventies. Until then the classical tradition of giving first priority to foreign affairs had been maintained; now international economic policy moved into first place. In the past a statesman in Europe had to win his spurs in foreign affairs; now this is no longer enough: it has to be underpinned by a knowledge of economic and currency matters.

Helmut Schmidt had studied economics in Hamburg and had become Senator there. After Karl Schiller's resignation in 1972 he ran the super-Ministry of Economics and Finance and in the same year he was made Minister of Finance with extended responsibility. As Chancellor his reputation as an expert on international economic and currency matters was undisputed, and his efforts to stabilize politics won him the respect of all parties at home.

The change of priorities in favour of world economics could be seen on the margins of the Helsinki Conference in August 1975. Helmut Schmidt got Gerald Ford, Valéry Giscard d'Estaing and Harold Wilson to agree to meet as soon as possible in order to discuss economic and currency problems. This was the basis for a new institution which has since become indispensable: the economic summit. Apart from the four premiers who had met together in Helsinki, the other members were Italy, Japan, and Canada.

The first economic summit took place in November of 1975 at Rambouillet; the next in June 1976 in Puerto Rico; this was followed in May 1977 by a summit meeting in London where President Carter made his first European appearance. He pleaded for more government borrowing in order to get the economy going and prevent unemployment from becoming a permanent phenomenon. He wanted the Federal Republic and Japan to be the 'locomotive' for the world economy. Schmidt energetically disagreed: investment, he said, depends on confidence, and there can be no confidence without stability. Schmidt dominated the scene in London with his arguments, with his analyses and his persuasiveness; eventually he won the necessary support for his point of view.

Rambouillet had paved the way for a reform of the currency system; the next conference at Puerto Rico was mainly devoted to relations with developing countries. Schmidt was the driving force behind the effort to discover what needed to be done, first, in order to stabilize the raw materials markets; and secondly, in order to discover what effect this would have on the developing countries themselves, and then on the industrial countries and the East. Bonn wanted to fix the market for seventeen different kinds of raw materials and to study the effect on a hundred developing nations and twenty-five industrial nations.

In the Federal Republic, where one out of every four jobs depends on exports, world economic policy is a vital question. In 1975 the developing countries exported 60 billion DM worth of goods to the Federal Republic, their largest European market, more than twice as much as in 1971. Between 1950 and 1974 Bonn spent 82 billion DM on co-operation with developing countries, half of this sum being from public funds. But then the FRG also imports half her raw materials from developing countries; in some cases, such as tin, 100 per cent comes from the Third World.

Fired by the success of the OPEC cartel, the countries of the Third World hoped that by adopting a similar policy with their raw materials they too could turn the world economy upside down. But this very soon turned out to be a utopian dream. They did, however, succeed in hammering the importance of the question into the heads of the politicians.

In the 1970s a new problem made its appearance. Perhaps not quite as serious as the problem of East/West relations but, still, a new spectre on the horizon: the problem of North/South relations.

Until then the security of the Federal Republic had been regarded solely as a military and political matter. The oil crisis made everybody realize the importance of the countries exporting raw materials. The Federal Republic has become the greatest exporter of industrial products in the world, and so she depends more than any other country on a free and prosperous world economy, and that of course includes good relations with her partners in the Third World. That is why the Bonn government, and especially Foreign Secretary

169

Genscher, are so keen on achieving a united EEC foreign policy towards the Middle East and Africa.

It was only after the Russian invasion of Afghanistan, a thrust in the direction of the Persian Gulf, that the industrialized countries of the West realized that although NATO guarantees their security in Europe, their prosperity as well as their survival depend on the vast, disturbed area outside the Atlantic Pact. Since then much discussion has taken place on how to achieve more security for this part of the world. The Federal Republic however feels she should abstain from participating in any possible widening of the NATO sphere because that would cause more harm than good. A very clear picture of Helmut Schmidt's conception of the economic scene is provided by an interview he gave to Peter Jenkins of the London *Guardian* in the autumn of 1975. He said:

'I don't believe in the direction of investment by the State. I don't believe in the growth of bureaucracy. I don't believe in the economic wisdom of the State as regards industrial management.

If one asks oneself what are the true reasons for the differentiated development of societies and economies between the British and most ones on the Continent, I think it has something to do with the fact that British society, much more than the Scandinavian, German, Austrian, and Dutch societies, is characterized by a class-struggle type of society. This is true for both sides of the upper class as well as for the working classes. I think that the way in which organized Labour on the one hand and industrial management on the other had dealt with their problems is outmoded.'

And returning to the difference between Germany and Britain he ended: 'You have to treat workers as equal members of society. You have to give them the self-esteem which they can only have if they acquire responsibility. Then you will be able to ask the trade unions to behave and to abstain from those idiotic policies. Then they will accept some guidance from outsiders – from the government or the party or whatever it is. But as long as you maintain the damned class-ridden society of yours you will never get out of your mess.'

One begins to understand why he is more and more often referred to as 'Europe's only statesman'; but also why people occasionally call him 'the schoolmaster' or 'the sergeant-major'.

The elections to the Federal Assembly were due in the autumn of 1976. Schmidt is difficult to attack from the Right, since he is a determined market economist, against Leftist experiments, in favour of taking a firm line over terrorism, acknowledged to be the only man capable of making a correct analysis of economic facts and drawing the political consequences. As Federal Minister Hans Matthöfer triumphantly remarked, 'You can't classify him, because people like him really shouldn't be allowed to exist.'

1972 was the first time the SPD beat the CDU/CSU, but soon afterwards the mood changed, and in 1974 the ruling coalition struck a new low. This failure was not redeemed until 1976. Helmut Kohl had a great success as Opposition leader and the CDU/CSU once more became the strongest party. But Kohl's attempt to claim that this gave him the right to be Chancellor was doomed to failure: even before the elections the FDP had declared that it would remain in coalition with the SPD, so he would have had no chance of forming a majority.

In 1976 the SPD/FDP won a majority, but it was very small, only eight votes. And in the second chamber, the Federal Assembly, they had slid into a minority, because at the start of 1976 the SPD/FDP coalition in Hanover broke up. The sixty-seven-year-old Prime Minister Alfred Kubel wanted to retire, but his chosen successor failed in the election when three delegates abstained and a fourth voted for the CDU.

For a long time a quarrel had been simmering in the CDU/CSU over who was entitled to lead the Union and who was Adenauer's true successor. On an average over the years the CSU had never had more than fifty representatives in the Assembly, while the CDU had had about four times that number: but there is no doubt that Strauss, the leader of the CSU, is the most gifted among the conservative politicians. Besides, the Bavarians have always emphasized their special position: they call themselves 'Bavarian Free State', for instance, and do not acknowledge the constitution. So there was nothing out of the ordinary about their demand to lead the coalition.

After the 1972 elections the simmering quarrel had turned into an open fight. Strauss thought that if he had been a candidate for the Chancellorship the CDU/CSU could have won the election. He had always dropped hints about a fourth party; the threat was that he would establish the CSU on a Federal basis instead of keeping it confined to Bavaria. Now he began to threaten to split the Parliamentary Party. Kohl hit back. For weeks the battle raged in the Opposition, with mounting anger and fear. Part of what Strauss said in private to the Parliamentary Party in Kreuth became known, as did a speech he made to a Committee of the Young Conservatives during a training session. The CDU was highly indignant when this appeared in *Der Spiegel*, and no wonder, because Strauss had said of Kohl: 'He is utterly unfit for the job. He hasn't the character, nor the brains, nor the political capabilities necessary. He lacks everything a candidate for the Chancellorship should have.' He had then moved on to speaking of the 'political pygmies' of the CDU, 'who only worry about their constituencies, those pocket-sized dwarves, those public relations politicians. . . . When an army has attacked three times on the wrong front and still hasn't realized that it must attack somewhere else for a change, then that's it. And believe you me, Helmut Kohl will never be Chancellor. When he's ninety he'll write his memoirs: "For forty years I was a candidate for the Chancellorship – lessons and experiences of a bitter period." Perhaps he'll write the last chapter in Siberia or somewhere.'

Kohl delivered an ultimatum: either the CSU must return to the ranks of the Parliamentary Party, or be prepared to see the CDU marching into Bavaria. Strauss capitulated. He is always more determined in words than in deeds. And he was surely right because it is highly questionable whether his fourth party outside Bavaria would have won him more than he would have lost inside Bavaria if there had been a right-wing alternative to the CSU there.

Helmut Schmidt was lucky. The mighty battle of words that raged for weeks in the CDU/CSU absorbed much political attention which would otherwise have been concentrated on the Chancellor's worst defeat – the pensions disaster. True, the disaster was not the fault of Schmidt but of his Labour Minister Walter Arendt: nevertheless Schmidt was the target for anger, derision, and reproaches as bitter as 'betrayal of the electorate'. He took it all on the chin.

The débâcle came about in this way. During the period of reformist euphoria more and more social benefits had been introduced: flexible retirement age, children's allowances for students up to the age of twenty-seven, special higher pension rights and so on. One out of every three DM spent by the government was for welfare purposes. The health service, too, had grown so expensive that an ever increasing portion of the gross profits had to be spent on public health insurance. Because of the regular rise in wages during the preceding years, the social security income automatically went up too. Arendt therefore reckoned it would not be difficult to raise pensions. So before the autumn elections of 1976 the Chancellor promised that pensions would rise by 10 per cent on 1 July 1977. But then the recession came and unemployment spread; and the more people were out of work, the more contributions declined.

Arendt had based his calculations on a high growth rate and this also turned out to be a mistake. On the contrary, it appeared that if the pensions increase went through, the government would be short of 11 billion DM. When the new economic figures appeared in December, it became clear that during the four years from 1977 to 1980 national insurance would have a deficit of 83 billion DM. In the Federal Republic one in six of the population lives on a pension, so it is not surprising that every error of any magnitude instantly runs into figures of billions. The dismay in Bonn was great, and so was the indignation throughout the country. Constituents everywhere raged against their representatives, and the Chancellor's reputation as an economic expert was severely shaken.

In 1957 Konrad Adenauer had launched a great social improvement: index-related pensions. It meant that with an interval of three and a half years pensions would rise at the same rate as wages. Before the elections the interval had been reduced by six months. But the boom was followed by a recession, so in 1977 wages only rose by 7 per cent, while pensions went on rising by 11 per cent. There was no way of dealing with the disaster except by a more or less undesirable compromise. There was much wailing and gnashing of teeth, and the unions, normally the Chancellor's staunchest champions, were harsher than anyone in their criticism. To make matters worse, it became increasingly obvious, not only in the Federal Republic, but everywhere in the West, that a high rate of unemployment would be unavoidable for many years to come.

Nor was there any gleam of light on the horizon in foreign affairs. In the West *détente* was withering away: President Ford declared he would no longer use the word, he would banish it from his vocabulary. And in the East they were just beginning to build ramparts against the consequences of *détente*. The relationship between the two Germanies froze over, and 'demarcation' became the watchword of the SED. Wolf Biermann was expelled, the first of a long series of intellectuals who were to leave the other Germany. In his New Year address for 1977 Chancellor Schmidt said: 'We all believed that after we had solved the world economic crisis everything would go on as before. But particularly in the last months it has become clear that things will not be as they were before 1974.'

The year 1977 will always be associated with the growth of terrorism. It had begun in 1968 when anarchists staged a fire in a department store in Frankfurt. The aim, as Andreas

Baader and Gudrun Ensslin later said at their trial, was 'to destroy a fetish of the consumer society'. In the beginning they deliberately waged war only on objects, but they soon abandoned such limitations. Two years later Ulrike Meinhof is said to have declared: 'We say that types in uniform are pigs; they're not human beings, and so we have to confront them. . . . And of course shooting is OK.'

1977 began with explosions in American installations and several policemen were shot. Eventually the first terrorist organization, the RAF (Red Army Fraction), was neutralized by means of massive planned counter-measures. Meanwhile the 'Second of June' Movement was formed in Berlin, and was responsible for the murder of President of the Court of Appeal von Drenkmann; in Heidelberg there was the 'Socialist Patients' Collective'; and when that was wiped out, new and smaller groups sprouted from the earth like mushrooms. A bomb was placed in the car of Federal Judge Buddenberg; bombs were thrown at the houses of his colleagues, and more policemen were murdered.

It became increasingly difficult to fight the terrorists because meanwhile a number of lawyers had identified with their cause. They kept communications open between the prisoners and the outside world, so that at times the prisons became the command centres from which operations were directed. In the meantime, an international terrorist network had developed, which made investigations even more difficult. Nevertheless the secret services and the police could claim some remarkable successes.

In the course of 1977 the terrorists in the Federal Republic started going for selective targets. Like the Ustachis in Yugoslavia and the Jewish Irgun in Palestine in the past, they attacked VIPs. In April the Federal Attorney General Siegfried Buback, his driver, and a policeman were shot; in July there was a particularly vicious attack on Jürgen Ponto, the Chairman of the second largest bank in the Federal Republic: he was shot by a young girl who presented him with a bouquet of roses; in October they killed the President of the Federal

Union of Employers, Hanns Martin-Schleyer. There was much argument: 'Yes,' one party said, 'we need tougher laws – we must stop the disastrous liberalization of the penal laws.' 'No,' said their opponents; 'we must not protect the rule of law to the point of killing it and turning ourselves into a police state.' Finally an incident occurred which mesmerized the whole German public for 106 hours: in October 1977 an aeroplance with eighty-six passengers was hijacked. The affair ended at Mogadishu, Somalia, with a brilliantly planned liberation manœuvre carried out with incredible precision by GSG 9, a special force troop.

It was a situation which threatened the whole State, because it severely shook people's confidence in the State's power to protect them. Mogadishu earned Helmut Schmidt the approval of all classes and parties to an extent no other Prime Minister has ever known. Seven thousand letters were received by the Chancellor's Office, and a poll showed that 58 per cent of those questioned had complete confidence in Schmidt.

In a prime-ministerial statement on the liberation of the hostages and the assassination of Hanns Martin-Schleyer, Schmidt declared with great and not particularly typical modesty: 'A man knows that whatever happens, whatever he does, and however hard he tries, he will not feel completely free from sins of omission and a sense of guilt: therefore no one can say he has done everything, and that everything he did was right.' The statement ended with the words: 'There will be opportunities for the Federal government to explain its reasons – and its doubts – in public. We accept that responsibility for the future. God help us.'

Der Spiegel wrote: 'Eventually the pent-up tension of the hostage affair dissolved with the shedding of a few tears; Chancellor Schmidt would prefer this not to have been so, though he himself affirmed it that very evening: "I should not have admitted it, but that is how it was."'

A few days later he was asked what could be learnt from the whole affair. By this time the psychological strain was beginning to recede, and he said: 'We learned that it pays to stand up for one another ... that a democratic state is not a State to be shat upon, a State to put up with everything that happens; we also learnt that one needs to keep one's cool even in extreme situations.' Another time he replied: 'What you learn is this: to combine optimal patience with utter concentration.' In the very week the passenger plane *Landshut* was freed in Mogadisu, three leading terrorists, Andreas Baader, Jan Carl Raspe, and Gudrun Ensslin, committed suicide with guns that had been smuggled into their prison.

The approval and admiration engendered by Mogadishu even prevailed during the Hamburg Party Conference in November 1977, otherwise the atomic energy crisis might have made things difficult for Schmidt. For while he stuck to his inaugural statement, 'We cannot give up developing our atomic energy programme. Atomic energy is necessary and essential to cover our foreseeable electricity requirements', the Party inclined to the opposite view. Schmidt got by with a compromise outlined in his speech: the problem of energy must be tackled 'without dogmatic options', he said, meaning we must use atomic energy, but only if nothing else will do. He carried off the victory in this internal Party conflict, and refrained from gloating. 'I stand in the centre of my Party', he assured the delegates. 'I was elected as a Social Democrat. You must trust my solidarity, and that you can do. I have to trust yours, and that I do.'

With the beginning of the Carter administration, certain difficulties in the field of foreign affairs set in whose complete significance was not to become apparent for several years. President Carter was basically a good man, honest, well intentioned, and seriously determined to live by noble maxims. But he was naïve and inexperienced. He was convinced that if one pursues good aims with all one's might one can achieve them. In his election campaign he had sworn that in contrast to Presidents Nixon and Ford he would concentrate on internal issues and not keep his eyes solely on foreign affairs, as they had done. But the first thing he did was to hurl himself at international problems, beginning, unfortunately, with the hardest of all: America's relations with the USSR.

He took over the government in January 1977; in March he sent his Secretary of state Cyrus Vance to Moscow with new suggestions for the SALT II agreement, negotiations for which were nearly complete. Vance returned with nothing achieved. Carter had previously announced that he was going to base his whole foreign policy on the question of human rights. There were certainly enough countries where human rights were trampled underfoot, from Idi Amin's Uganda through the South American military dictatorships to the countries of the Eastern bloc. If Carter had acted on his principles equally towards all of them, this might perhaps have been a welcome step. But for the moment he concentrated on the Soviet Union. He received Alexander Solzhenitsyn, he wrote personally to André Sacharov, he condemned the Soviet leaders. In short, he used human rights as a weapon to fight the USSR.

He did not have long to wait for the consequences. After only a few months the more important leaders of the four citizens' rights committees that had been set up in the Soviet Union after the Helsinki Conference were sent to prison or to labour camps. Never before had such committees or even activities been tolerated in the USSR – and now this rising hope had been dashed.

With far less talk about morality Henry Kissinger had achieved far more. Several times he had presented the Soviet Ambassador, Dobrynin, with a list of names and asked him to co-operate in getting the people on it released, because that would be taken as a sign of good will and would therefore help negotiations along. In this way Kissinger had managed to help thousands of Soviet citizens. Even Solzhenitsyn and Bukowsky had been allowed to leave the country as a result of Kissinger's methods. But such things, of course, were possible only through confidential conversations. As soon as the President of the United States began publicly to make conditions, demands, and even to issue what almost amounted to an ultimatum, the whole process broke down.

Carter was not only inexperienced: time was to show that he was also unchangeable, so that it was impossible to foretell what his reactions or plans were going to be: this was equally intolerable to his friends and his foes. Carter's behaviour undermined the one thing that was needed at this period of increasing complications: stability. Henry Kissinger's consistent policy had succeeded in showing the Soviets that in spite of their opposing ideologies the two sides have certain interests very much in common, and that these need fostering: namely stability and peace. Now the two Super-powers were negotiating without any concept or long-term plan, and without any co-ordination in the way they managed the crises that occurred.

In the autumn of 1979 Carter suddenly became vehemently disturbed over the Soviet brigade in Cuba, which he called 'unacceptable' although it had been stationed on the island for many years. Shortly after he calmed down again and accepted the situation. When the Russians marched into Afghanistan in December 1979 there was at first no reaction at all from Washington. But then Carter declared that the attack was the most dangerous incident that had occurred since the Second World War. Obviously the Soviet *coup* had taken him completely by surprise, just like the events in Iran, although in both cases there had been warning signals.

Some people will object that there is no point in making efforts to reach agreements with the Russians, since they only misuse them – by rearming for instance – but who says that only one of the Super-powers has the right to superior arms? It must be obvious that that is what they both want. In the Cuban crisis of 1962 the Americans forced the Russians to remove their rocket installations from the island: John McCloy negotiated with Kuznetsov on how this was to be done and with what controls. McCloy described what happened: 'Everything was carried out on time and precisely as we had agreed. At the time we were so strong and superior that the Russians had no other choice. When it was over we shook hands, and Kuznetsov said: "Well, Mr McCloy, you'll never find us in this situation again." By which he meant: such a thing will never happen to us again, in other words our power relationship will never be so unequal again.' There is no doubt that political balance and global stability depend, on the one hand, on maintaining a military equilibrium; but on the other – and this should never be forgotten – on constant contact and diplomatic activity. That is the only way one can hope to contain acute conflicts – and perhaps one day also to limit rearmament.

There is sense in the objection that the Soviet policy of supporting national liberation movements wherever in the world they may occur makes it impossible to aim for peace. In 1972, long before Angola, Mozambique, and the Horn of Africa, Brezhnev and Nixon agreed the following:

> The USA and the USSR are highly conscious of the importance of preventing situations which might lead to a dangerous deterioration in their relationship. Both sides acknowledge that efforts, whether direct or indirect, to gain an advantage at the expense of the other side are not in accordance with this goal.

When Brezhnev was in Bonn in May 1978 he and Schmidt issued a joint statement: 'Both sides consider it important that neither should have military superiority over the other. They are of the opinion that approximate parity and equality will be sufficient to secure their defences.' But the upshot is this: when opponents so deeply divided not only ideologically but also from the viewpoint of power politics have conversations of so general a character these can hardly be regarded as binding. It is not a question of agreements but of declarations of intent, or, more likely, of mood. So it is all the more important to remain in constant contact in order to contain specific conflicts and crises as they occur.

Carter's inconsistency had consequences for his relations with friendly Powers as well. Europeans have become more independent and able to act for themselves. They had no choice. They have all had sobering experiences of one kind or another. In the case of the Federal Republic it was over negotiations about the neutron bomb. In response to Carter's urging, Chancellor Schmidt had undertaken the arduous task of overcoming his Party's opposition to having the bomb stationed in Germany; but in the end when he had just succeeded it turned out that Carter had dropped the idea with the excuse that the Europeans could not make up their minds.

Early in 1979 the Federal Republic, or rather Helmut Schmidt, was invited for the first time to join the Summit Conference in Guadeloupe and make a fourth with the US, Great Britain and France. This showed that the two most important European nations, France and Great Britain, felt that they could no longer leave it to the USA to take the lead, and that the Europeans ought to move closer together. Even in America it was thought, as the *Financial Times* wrote at the time, 'that the alliance would be seriously and dangerously weakened without Germany's economic and military power, and also without her counsel and, in some respects, her example'.

Helmut Schmidt's prestige reached its climax in 1979. His reputation and the general and universal confidence he inspires are founded not least on the fact that never for a moment has he strayed from the three priorities which have always been on his programme: close friendship with the USA, a strong Atlantic Pact, and constant strengthening of the European Community. Sporadically fears are voiced in the West that Moscow would lure the Federal Republic away from her allies, but they have never been associated with the name of Helmut Schmidt.

The end of 1979 saw two major events whose effects were to reach well into the eighties: the NATO two track decision to step up armaments (if an agreement about arms control should not be reached), and the Soviet invasion of Afghanistan.

To understand the NATO decision, one must remember that from the very beginning Western defence policy was

based on the 'sword and shield' theory. The shield is represented by conventional weapons, where the Russians are
superior in strength to the West, therefore the transatlantic
sword – represented by intercontinental missiles – acts as a
supplementary deterrent. This concept has undergone a
number of changes in the course of time. In the beginning
'massive retaliation' was envisaged, the destruction of industrial complexes and big cities. Today the targets are more
precisely defined. The idea is to destroy the enemy's intercontinental missile bases. Both the Super-powers have vast
intercontinental striking capacity, and in addition the Soviets
have medium-range missiles which are placed so that one-
third are aimed at China and two-thirds at Europe.

According to an estimate of May 1981 by the London
International Institute for Strategic Studies (IISS), the Soviet
Union has at least 220 missiles of type SS–20, each with three
warheads and a range of 4400 kilometres. A year before there
were only 160 missiles. So sixty additional SS–20 missiles
were manufactured in the course of one year, an average of
one per week. In addition, most of the old SS–4s and SS–5s
with only one warhead (which were meant to be replaced by
the SS–20) have simply been left standing in their positions:
in the spring of 1981 there were still 390 of them aiming at
Europe. The launchers for the SS–20 were all built during the
past three or four years – during which time NATO made no
additions to the number of its missiles capable of hitting
Russian targets. And since Brezhnev in his conversations
with Schmidt in Bonn in May 1978 stated that there was
approximate equality between East and West, it follows that
today the balance has been destabilized.

Until recently the Western Powers have not thought it
necessary to introduce medium-range missiles to counter the
old SS–4s and SS–5s. Why then, one may ask, all this sudden
excitement? The answer is this: first of all the SS–20 is far
more dangerous, accurate, effective and also mobile, and
therefore harder to combat; secondly, the haste and assiduity
of Russian rearmament is disturbing; and thirdly, whereas

the American intercontinental capacity had previously been thought sufficient as a deterrent, even for Europe, this view has now become outmoded. The SALT agreement lays down that both Super-powers should have the same number of intercontinental missiles (ICBMS) so that they neutralize one another. Theoretically, there then would be no deterrence left against the Russian medium-range rockets aiming at Europe. So the balance between East and West has been destroyed in favour of the East, because in addition to their superiority in conventional weapons they are now also superior in medium-range atomic weapons.

The idea behind the NATO decision of December 1979 is to redress the balance by means of negotiations, or, if they should fail, to introduce medium-range missiles in the West. For if the imbalance becomes too great, so the argument runs, then the Western deterrent loses its credibility, and the temptation to take advantage of this situation may be too strong for the other side. Therefore if it should become necessary 572 medium-range missile systems (Pershing–2 and cruise missiles) were to be installed in Western Europe.

A few months previously Helmut Schmidt had stopped off at Moscow on his way to Tokyo. He used the opportunity to urge the Russian leaders to stop their medium-range rearmament, otherwise NATO would be forced to rearm as well. The Soviets paid no attention to his warning. It was chiefly Schmidt who insisted on linking the decision to step up armaments with an offer to negotiate with Moscow. And it had also been Schmidt who, in a lecture to the IISS in London in 1977, drew attention to Soviet superiority in the field of medium-range missiles, which he described as a threat to *détente*. He now hopes that the threat to step up armaments will finally induce the Russians and Americans alike to negotiate seriously in order to preserve *détente* in the heart of Europe. At the start of the eighties, however, the resistance within his own Party against the NATO decision has become so strong that it will take all his vigour and cunning to get it through in 1983.

The second event of far-reaching, long-term importance was the Russian invasion of Afghanistan in December 1979. The whole world was indignant that a Third World country should be attacked in time of peace and hundreds of thousands of the inhabitants forced to flee.

Eighteen months later there were 1.8 million Afghan refugees in Pakistan – 10 per cent of Afghanistan's population. At the UN 104 nations voted for a resolution protesting against the attack and demanding immediate withdrawal. A conference of the Islamic nations was specially called and voted likewise. Never had Moscow been criticized so unanimously and with so much disgust all over the world.

Washington pulled out all the stops. Carter blocked the export of all grain in excess of the 8 million tons negotiated by Kissinger in a long-term agreement: he placed an embargo on electronic and oil-producing equipment, and he advised the American Olympic Committee not to go to Moscow for the summer Olympics unless the Russians withdrew from Afghanistan by 20 February; he also allocated more expenditure for defence. He urged his European allies to follow his example, putting special emotional pressure on the Federal Republic. Bonn cancelled all exports to Russia except those which, like the American grain shipments, depended on long-term agreements; and although the Federal Republic was the only major nation to boycott the Olympic Games, she was singled out for frequent reproaches that she had not shown sufficient solidarity.

Mrs Thatcher immediately declared herself in accord with the Americans and was therefore regarded as an especially devoted ally, in spite of the fact that the British Olympic team subsequently went to Moscow after all. This shows how much importance the Americans attach to verbal protestations. The German sportsmen were not allowed to go, and yet Helmut Schmidt was accused of slacking, because he advised the German National Olympic Committee who had to make the final decision that they should give the Russians until 15 May (the last registration date for the Olympics) to leave Afghanistan, instead of 20 February, the date chosen by Carter.

In a statement of 20 March 1980, Schmidt said: 'The proper conditions still do not exist, because the occupation of Afghanistan and the constant fighting there continue unabated. But the beginnings of the Olympic idea in classical Greece are indissolubly associated with peace among the nations. Unless peace is restored in Afghanistan, the consequences will be inevitable.' So there was never any question of going or not going: the idea was first of all to give the Russians until the last possible moment to withdraw; and secondly to show that Germany's decision depended on her own initiative, and not on orders from the USA.

The Federal Republic soon began to feel the post-Afghanistan frost. Immediately after his return from Moscow in January Erich Honecker cancelled a planned meeting with the Federal Chancellor. The Czechs politely disinvited Foreign Secretary Genscher, and the Hungarian Foreign Secretary regretted that he would have to postpone his visit to Bonn which was due to take place in the same week. The Economic Secretary Count Lambsdorff did not travel to Poland, as planned, and the Labour Secretary Ehrenberg did not go to Moscow.

Bonn had hoped to be able to maintain *détente* at least in Europe, but this began to become increasingly doubtful. The only thing Schmidt managed to achieve was to persuade the US Deputy Secretary of State Warren Christopher when he came to Bonn that it would be highly counter-productive to extend NATO protection as far as the Indian Ocean and to send German warships to support the US Navy in the Persian Gulf: such steps would only provoke the Soviets to further expansion.

For experience has taught us that, as in the Theatre of the Absurd, East and West have for many years been engaged in a macabre play: as soon as one side places a black piece in any part of the world, the other immediately puts a white one down beside it: and so the chain reaction goes on and on. But unlike draughts or checkers which are only played at the concrete level of the board, the international game is played at an emotional level ruled by imagination, suspicion, and fear. So the question, Who plays the last piece? tends to receive a subjective instead of an objective reply.

In the case of Afghanistan the Soviets apparently thought that the signs pointed to an American move there in order to free their hostages in Iran. The idea of having the Americans as neighbours in addition to the Chinese and the inscrutable Khomeini was evidently too much for the Russians. They thought they were preventing the Americans from establishing a new base, and they were hoist with their own petard. A year later, if they had had to decide between Afghanistan and Poland, they would doubtless have considered Poland much more important.

So the cold breath of the cooling Super-blocs blew across Central Europe too. But the Russians did not cancel Helmut Schmidt's planned visit to Moscow. The Chancellor talked it over with the other Allies: they were not enthusiastic, probably because they feared that in his efforts to preserve *détente* he might go too far; on the other hand they did not want to be responsible for his refusal to go: so in July 1980 he set out for the Soviet capital.

He had asked for as many members as possible of the Politbureau to be invited to the obligatory gala dinner. Except for two who were stationed in far-off regions they all appeared. Schmidt had seen to it that translations of his speech were distributed before he made it, so that those present could follow his words. When he spoke his mind on the subject of Afghanistan, Suslov, the ideological eminence in the Politbureau, who was sitting beside him, suddenly slapped his typescript down on the table. A few others followed his example and laid down their copies though not quite as noisily and demonstratively.

In my mind's eye I could see the Chancellor of the little Federal Republic standing in the great Kremlin surrounded by the mighty members of the Politbureau, and interrupting his account I said: 'You must have felt jolly nervous?' 'And how! I think from that moment I read much faster in order to get it over as soon as possible.' 'And what happened at the end?' 'For a few seconds there was a frightening silence – then Brezhnev clapped, and they all joined in.'

I myself was in Washington at the time, and when I went to the State Department next morning they said with great admiration, 'Your Chancellor made a very courageous speech.' Nothing else directly resulted from Schmidt's trip, but those who believed in *détente* were glad, while the sceptics saw that the bear does not instantly devour everyone who enters his cave, and that one can go there without automatically relinquishing one's own interests.

The postponed meeting between Schmidt and Honecker was now to take place at Rostock in August. The advance party was already there to make all the preparations, when the visit was called off – this time by Bonn. The SED had expressed a wish to alter the programme of the visit and to cancel a visit to the port altogether. Apparently there had been several protest demonstrations about food shortages in Rostock. Meanwhile unrest was increasing in Poland, and the SED probably feared that it would spread to the GDR. So after careful consideration, Bonn decided to cancel the visit.

Meanwhile the 1980 election campaign had already got under way in the Federal Republic. In July 1979 the CDU/CSU had nominated Franz Josef Strauss as their candidate for the Chancellorship. Now people were looking forward with great excitement to the duel between the two great matadors, Strauss and Schmidt; they are, after all, the most powerful figures in Bonn. Both are political thoroughbreds, as the expression goes, both great orators, swift in repartee, highly knowledgeable; and both can be brutal demagogues when necessary. The popular press began to compare the biographies of the two men, their sayings, their attitude to various problems, their incomes, eating habits, life styles, and what they read and write. Curious parallels came to light between two such completely dissimilar men.

Both had shone at school and done brilliantly in all their examinations. Both had spent the war in anti-aircraft units. Both had written three best sellers each. Both had begun as Ministers for Defence and moved on to Finance. Both are convinced that knowledge is power. Schmidt had already studied economics and monetary policy when he began to settle into a completely new field: night after night he studied everything he could find connected with security matters, and then wrote three standard works on the subject. Strauss studied classics; he had already held three ministerial posts when he went to Innsbruck to study public law and monetary policy. From 1965 onwards he was a successful expert on finance at the Federal Assembly, and finally, in the great coalition, he became Minister of Finance.

Both men are self-confident and let no one dictate to them. Schmidt: 'I don't talk rubbish, I speak my mind.' Strauss: 'I am what I am. I don't care a damn about anything else. No one is going to make me dance to their tune.' *Das Bild* compared their incomes, and found that Strauss was better off by 2000 DM.

It is astonishing that two men with so many gifts in common – intelligence, oratory, energy, ambition, vitality – can also be so different. It is worth taking a look at them both from this point of view.

Schmidt's fundamental position is democratic, even if he can sometimes seem brusque and intolerant. He likes working in a team, is passionately fond of debating, and enjoys listening – at least, if what is being said is interesting. He has the qualities that make a statesman: he is sharp and precise in his analyses, he knows how to judge what is possible in any given circumstance, he is decisive, and finally he possesses the persuasiveness and power of exposition to convince people that his decisions are the right ones.

He himself confesses that his judgements always start with an instinctive reaction, which he then works out rationally and pragmatically in his own mind, before testing it in conversations with his friends and with experts. Quoting Max

Weber he says a politician needs three qualities: passion, a sense of responsibility, and a sense of proportion; and off his own bat he adds: intuition, eloquence, and moral courage. Hostile critics often describe him as a schoolmaster and say there is no point in talking to him because after five minutes he starts lecturing you. He is 'an ungracious knowall', they say.

It is true that Helmut Schmidt has his share of arrogance, but he is disarmingly frank about it. Once when an interviewer asked him whether he did not miss having a team to work with or at least an intellectual equal with whom to talk things over, he replied, 'No, I'm quite intelligent enough myself. What I need is an official to control me.' And on another occasion, 'I am not perfectly satisfied with my party neither are they with me. But I can't find a better party and they can't find a substitute for me.'

This somewhat ironical statement illustrates the special dual quality of Schmidt's intellect. He has all the intellectual's powers of analysis, but at the same time he has the practical active intelligence that knows how and where things should be done. And he carries in his own breast an indispensable grain of doubt, which makes things harder for him, but acts as a useful corrective to his occasionally alarming self-assurance.

Schmidt likes to call himself the leading employee of the German Federal Republic. His fear of sentimentality leads him to prefer dry and sometimes brusque terms of expression. Berthold Beitz, head of the Krupp firm, says about him: 'He is on the same wavelength as the people in industry, like two cog wheels interlocking. You could put him in charge of Krupp or Hapag-Lloyd and he would do very well indeed.' Schmidt himself had this to say on the subject: 'The Opposition leader misses intellectual leadership in the country? I don't believe the State should be an ideas factory, let alone the government.' Manufacturing ideas, he thinks, is the business of philosophers and writers, of universities and churches. Three years ago three intellectuals, Fritz Raddatz,

Siegfried Lenz, and Günter Grass, set out to crucify the un-intellectual 'manager' in an interview which was later printed in *Die Zeit*: afterwards everyone agreed that the only one to come unscathed out of the ordeal was Schmidt.

The conversation was started with the assertion by one of the interviewers that social democracy – meaning of course Schmidt himself – was reactionary in its attitude to the arts and mistrustful of intellectuals. Schmidt is especially inter-ested in paintings, worships Henry Moore, plays the organ and piano, and is an omnivorous reader. Quite rightly he describes himself as an intellectual. He replied:

'In recent years the tendency has become increasingly marked for everyone in our society to aspire to higher education. If that is going to mean that only academically trained voices will be heard at local party gatherings, and that the workers will be unable to have their say, then I should be horrified. It would really frighten me.'

'And why, if you don't mind?'

'It would not be fair to narrow down culture to the fabrications of the intellectuals. In past centuries great artists have usually begun as craftsmen. That was true of the great Italian painters over several centuries; it is true of Veit Stoss and Tilman Rie-menschneider, of the great cathedral builders in Northern France and in Germany, of the builders of Gothic brick architecture all along the Baltic coast – to give only a few examples. So culture existed and continues to exist without any need for intellectuals to play a leading part in it. Though it is true that in many cases great, talented, and divinely gifted artists have become intellec-tuals in the course of their lives.'

The interviewers maintained that Schmidt set no example, that he neglected cultural matters. One of them said provo-catively: 'Well-intentioned people may say that he hides his light under a bushel. But that leads to the question: is there a light at all? Or only a bushel?' This was Schmidt's reply:

'I feel sorry for the members of the German intelligentsia who think that whoever happens to be Chancellor has the duty to educate the people culturally. It's not his duty at all. Neither is it his duty to set the philosophical tone for modern society. Just as you would be very reluctant to accept the government as a culture Pope, so you must get rid of the notion that the government should use its powers to encourage whatever art form you favour at a given moment. That is not the job of the German Federal government. On the contrary: the constitution deliberately forbids the government to have a cultural policy – to the extent that we have the greatest difficulty in getting the ten *Länder* of the Federation to agree to set up a National Foundation.

Helmut Schmidt is well aware of the heavy mortgage on Germany from the Hitler period. This is always present in his mind. It was only in conjunction with President Giscard d'Estaing and under Giscard's protection that he recently began to discard partially the role of a 'political dwarf'. In view of this careful behaviour it seems incomprehensible that he finds it so difficult to suppress certain derogatory remarks about other people. His relationship with President Carter was poisoned by this habit.

But if Helmut Schmidt sometimes lets himself go, Franz Josef Strauss lets himself go all the time. It is partly spontaneity and temperament, partly the pleasure of self-assertion, of fighting, of being better than others, or bashing on. Strauss' behaviour springs both from his total commitment to whatever he happens to be thinking or doing and from a lack of reserve and perspective. When his speeches don't begin with a thunder clap they gradually build up to stormy rumblings. There is no real need to hunt out the secret minutes of private meetings of the CSU which turn up from time to time, though no one can tell how authentic they are: it is quite enough to read his official speeches. In October 1959, for instance, Strauss had said in a speech at Hollfield that the West could 'wipe out' the Soviet Union. At the Party Conference in Berlin in May 1980 he said:

> The men in power in the Kremlin are masters of the game; but they are not playing against Helmut Schmidt: he is just a pawn in their game.... His general incapacity and lack of scruples are

such that he lets the Soviets make use of him in their propaganda to intimidate the West.

The candidate for the Chancellorship had many names for the acting Chancellor: 'a megalomaniac', 'a person fit for a mental home', 'the war Chancellor', 'an instrument of Russian psychological warfare'. 'If ridiculousness could kill, I shouldn't have an opponent.'

No other politician has spent so long in the limelight as Strauss did and no one has been as controversial – the epitome of all evil to some and a much admired genius to others, but always a caricature, a cliché of himself. Strauss entered politics as soon as he left the army. He helped to found the CSU whose Secretary he became in 1948. He has been a delegate to the Federal Assembly since 1949, when he was thirty-three. At thirty-four he became Deputy Leader of the Parliamentary Party, at thirty-eight Minister without Portfolio, at forty-one Secretary for Defence.

Such a talented and highly educated politician (in the Assembly only Carlo Schmid had more academic qualifications than he) must be saddened by the fact that his ascent, so vigorously begun, never led to the highest peak. But it is not untypical of the man that when in 1979 he finally decided to stand for the Chancellorship, he regretted his decision the very next day and was tempted to withdraw.

Strauss has a phenomenal memory, but he tends to forget that he has frequently changed his mind. At the time when he worshipped de Gaulle he was often an outspoken critic of the USA. It was he who turned the Federal government (then in the hands of the CDU) against Washington's policy of *détente*. He fought against the treaty to ban atomic warfare, 'a new Versailles, on a cosmic scale this time'. He dreamt of an independent European atomic force: 'For German policy to be totally linked to American policy would not only hamper the scope of Germany's policy but it would make it a function of American politics; it would also delay – if not prevent – Europe's integration into a political unity.'

Today Strauss declares that Schmidt's 'so-called policy for peace' means relaxing Germany's ties with America and that it is mortally dangerous. During his election campaign he also pointed out that Schmidt had once voted in the Federal Assembly against setting up the *Wehrmacht* and against joining NATO. He has evidently forgotten that in 1949 he himself made the famous remark, 'If anyone wants to pick up a gun again – may his hand drop off.' When asked about this statement in April 1964 by Günter Gaus, Strauss replied, 'I should have wished our country not to be faced with this necessity until a later stage.... We needed a period of convalescence after the exaggerated militarism, the perversion of power as a political tool, after the literal demoralization of our politics through the worship of naked, brutal force.'[46]

Strauss is no Nazi, no Fascist, as his enemies often declare. And he never was. His Catholic upbringing and his father saved him from becoming a member of the Nazi Party. He may be more powerful and determined in words than in deeds, but he is not a coward, as his opponents also claim. As a thirty-year-old lieutenant in Russia he refused to obey an order to advance his battery without infantry protection. The refusal might easily have cost him his head, but it saved the lives of his lancers.

His great handicaps are lack of self-control and lack of psychological judgement. Whenever a speech by Strauss is announced, no matter in what part of the Republic, people flock to hear him. They want to hear him not because they expect new insights, but because there are always fun and games: no one else hurls such splendid insults, no one else goes so recklessly into the attack.

The election campaign of 1980 for the Federal Assembly was of necessity distinguished by much personality mongering. Strauss concentrated entirely on attacking socialism on the grounds that its home policy destroys the order of free politics and its foreign policy leads to capitulating to the Communists. By comparison he made little of the government's frequently slapdash approach to economic and financial matters, which would have been a far more useful target for the Opposition to attack.

The coalition retaliated by branding Strauss as a danger to peace, or simply as a danger. Genscher, the leader of the third party, the FDP, was naturally anxious to impress his own party's personality on the voters as third parties always must: but with the clash of personalities in the duel between Schmidt and Strauss it was difficult for him to represent a third point of view. Nevertheless, he emerged as victor in the elections. Of course this was mainly because there were many members of the CDU/CSU who did not want to vote for Strauss and who were for Schmidt but against the SPD; these people voted for Genscher.

Thanks to the big rise in FDP votes the coalition won a majority of forty-five seats. Large majorities are, of course, always made up of many different groups, and all of them are therefore tempted to ride their hobby horses. When Brandt had his big electoral victory in the autumn of 1972 it was exactly the same. In the elections in Nordrhein–Westphalia in May 1980 the FDP had not even reached the 5 per cent mark necessary for sending a member to the Assembly in the *Land* with the largest population. Therefore the victory of the FDP in the Federal election in autumn was a shot in the arm for their self-confidence.

Genscher is the most powerful Foreign Secretary in the Western world. He is not only a cabinet Minister and therefore dependent on the Premier, the Premier is equally dependent on him, because he is the leader of the FDP. When the White House gets tired of Alexander Haig they can get rid of him; that can't happen to Genscher, because the Bonn coalition would break apart.

In foreign policy the two coalition chiefs, Schmidt and Genscher, play different roles. The difference springs not so much from deliberate intentions as from their very different nature. Schmidt is acknowledged to be 100 per cent in favour of the Atlantic connection; but he always strives to keep the dialogue going with Moscow, because he knows that that is necessary in order to protect Berlin which is always potentially under threat, and secondly because it is the only way to prevent or contain crises before they become too serious. Besides, he does not care for ideological motives or arguments. Schmidt is convinced that the two different social systems which are also rivals for power can co-exist peacefully only if their reactions and policies are mutually predictable. But how can this be unless they are constantly in contact with one another?

Genscher is equally convinced that the freedom of the Federal Republic is indissolubly linked to the American alliance; but having been born in Saxony he is possibly not quite as assiduous in his efforts to preserve and develop good relations with the Communists. This is the reason why for many years he was regarded with displeasure in the East.

The autumn 1980 elections were immediately followed by something of a hang-over. The hobby horses were not yet saddled, but a problem previously suppressed now loomed up before the Ministers responsible for the economy: the country's financial crisis. The reasons were plain to see: low growth rates, high oil prices, huge debts, increased unemployment, the heavy burden of a welfare state.

The Minister for Economic Affairs, Count Lambsdorff, called for greater productivity. Otto Wolff von Amerongen, the President of the Confederation of Industry and Commerce, called for people to stop thinking that the State would provide. The President of the Central Bank, Karl-Otto Pöhl, issued gloomy prognoses of the future. He too called for increased productivity on the one hand, and for moderation of demands on the other. Everywhere programmes were cancelled or curtailed, and the government promised to close down some of its own operations and to thin out the jungle of subsidies.

But reducing subsidies requires courage and persistence, because the more firms find themselves in the red the harder it is to resist appeals for help and protection from starving industries. Germany is practically the only European country that still clings to the principle of free trade. No one, no Ministry – except perhaps the Defence Ministry – will remain unscathed. And suddenly everyone notices that the State has spread too wide and that it is not exactly the most economical of housewives.

All these problems are not just for the time being. We shall be saddled with them for several years. The new budget in the beginning of 1982 has demanded cuts in every sphere. We shall see over the years whether the social consensus which has hitherto underpinned peace and prosperity in the Republic will survive the necessary cuts. When there is nothing left to hand out, governing becomes much more difficult. Knives are being sharpened on all sides: in the Federal government, in the *Länder*, and in local government. And no one can say what will happen in view of the steadily increasing financial demands within the Alliance. In 1980 the Federal Republic paid 5 billion DM net more into the EEC kitty than she received.

On top of all this the bitter controversy about energy policy and increasing armaments has not even reached its climax. Everything at once is coming down on the government in Bonn. The Chancellor has long kept silent on the subject of the financial situation, the quarrels within the Party, the revolt of left-wingers against the decision to step up armaments, and also in answer to complaints about pacificism, neutralism, and anti-Americanism. Inside and outside Germany the diagnosis is the same: loss of authority. The commentaries are pitiless. Many people talk of the government as though it had already ceased to exist. They think that the situation is similar to what it was with Ludwig Erhard in 1966 or with Willy Brandt in 1974. And indeed, one does ask oneself whether the stress of the last few years has been too much for Schmidt? Why does he not come down on the rebels and malcontents with fire and sword as he used to do?

Only in May 1981, before the trip to his first meeting with President Reagan, did the storm break in two speeches, one at the Party Conference of the Bavarian SPD at Wolfratshausen, the other two days earlier at Recklinghausen. A sub-district had applied to withdraw its consent to the rearmament decision. The Chancellor described the dangers of political blackmail by the Russians with their arsenal of missiles. Since 1945 too many nations had learnt that 'the Soviets don't follow the precepts of the Sermon on the Mount'. If the views expressed by the sub-district were to spread to the whole party, 'then I should not be able to go on carrying the responsibility for the Federal government'. He had already anticipated this formal warning of his resignation at Recklinghausen, and had staked his political future on the Western Alliance and the Federal Republic's security policy. 'I stand or fall with the implementation of the NATO decision – and not just with the *start* of negotiations, but with their successful *conclusion*.'

That very day thousands demonstrated against the decision to step up armaments. One of the rebellious Left in the Federal Assembly who later left the SPD, Manfred Coppik, at a rally in Frankfurt said that although the Russian armaments policy was open to much criticism, in the present situation, 'it is US policy that is the greatest threat to peace'. Helmut Schmidt's reaction at Wolfratshausen to such statements was to 'almost scream with rage', as the papers reported: 'Stop allowing yourselves to be conned into thinking that the Americans are our enemies and the Russians our friends.' Once more he outlined the principles on which the Federal Republic must insist: military and political equilibrium between the blocs, containment of conflict, control of crises, *détente*, and a predictable policy on the part of Bonn.

The peace movement that was such a headache to him had spread with exceptional speed through the Federal Republic. Leftists, the Green Front, and Christians are all united by the same motives: fear of war, protest against the waste of financial resources, and a desire to do more for the Third World.

The largest organization is the Krefelder Appeal. In November 1980 a forum was held at Krefeld to discuss the motion

'Atomic death threatens us all: no more atomic missiles in Europe'. Invitations to the forum had come from the DFU (German Peace Union), a communist-influenced body whose leaders had just returned from a visit to the Soviet Union and the GDR. By the beginning of 1982 they had collected one million signatures. But the chief impetus comes not from the communists, but from the anger and disgust many people feel for what seems an absurd arms race that has gone on for thirty years without providing more security to either side. As all the elections in the Federal Republic showed, the Communists on their own are no longer inspiring, they are too weak to initiate anything. Thus they have to infiltrate independent movements. They stoke up the fire in such movements, but they do not originate them. And the vast majority of those who demonstrate for peace, try to keep away the Communists. This certainly was the case with those 300,000 who gathered in Bonn in October 1981.

Resistance against rearmament does not need to be artificially created, it is all too easily comprehensible. Thirty years ago, in 1952, Adenauer argued that if we work with all our might to build ourselves a strong military position, then the Russians will realize that there's no point in going on, and they will give in. Since then no one has given in. But in 1982, according to a report by the SIPRI Institute in Stockholm, the world will be spending $550 billion on armaments. So it is legitimate to ask: is this costly, never-ending race to go on *ad infinitum*, even if everything else goes to pieces? Shall we reach a point where nothing will flourish except the arms industry? This is what many young people ask themselves.

The real question is: can the arms race be stopped? And who can stop it? The Russians are much too suspicious and their inferiority complex is much too great for them to take such a step. The historian and Russian specialist George Kennan has pointed out that also in the nineteenth century the Russians aroused surprise and anxiety in every European cabinet because their army was always much larger than was needed for defence purposes, at least by Western standards.

Therefore we cannot expect them today to have the courage to stop the armaments spiral of their own accord. Today, where they cannot feed themselves without help from outside; where their technology is a long way behind the technology of the West as is the productivity of their economy. Politically, too, they have a serious handicap: their western territories border on nations in a state of unrest who all would like to leave the Warsaw Pact and rather join the other side; in an age of nationalist revival, nationalism within their own borders presents a problem too; they regard the Chinese as a colossal threat and feel encircled by enemies. After Afghanistan they have lost all their friends in the Third World, who regard the Soviet Union as an imperialistic power; their ideology has long since forfeited the persuasiveness and the promise of salvation that it once possessed. The one area in which they are immensely strong is the military. No wonder they cling to that and try to make it ever stronger at the expense of the economy and the people's welfare: their weakness in every other area is so great that they can never catch up with the West, let alone, as Khrushchev used to believe, surpass it.

So it could be dangerous for the West to step up its armaments and deprive the Soviets of their only advantage: their leaders might begin to wonder whether the best thing would not be to make a pre-emptive strike to attack before the other side can start a preventive war and while they themselves still have the advantage. For we must never lose sight of the fact that all signals from the West, and also the rhetoric from Washington, will be interpreted by the Russians to mean that the West wants to force them to capitulate.

During the Second World War the Russians relied on the friendship pact concluded with Hitler in 1939. When Hitler's armies overran them in 1942 they were unprepared and could not prevent his advance to the outskirts of Leningrad and Moscow nor the death of twenty million Russians in the war. Today they are determined that this shall never happen again. That is another fact we must take into account for it means that their thinking is concentrated more on defence than on offence in Europe.

So the initiative to stop the worldwide armaments race must come from the West. Negotiations on arms control are indispensable. Only by controlled disarming will the world become safer, not by more arms. Helmut Schmidt has insisted on talks, and to him the credit is principally due that both sides eventually agreed to go to Geneva: perhaps this is the first time in fifty years that also for financial reasons everyone is equally interested in arms control. But we must be clear about one thing: there is no point in this undertaking unless the West is willing to negotiate without trying to force the Russians to surrender, and without any idea of punishing them for this or that.

The beginning of the eighties has proved to be turbulent for the coalition. Twelve years of heavy responsibility have left their mark on the SPD as well as the FPD. Both parties are deeply split, both are rent by struggles about fundamental directions. This became very apparent during the budget debates. And since only present triumphs count in politics, not past ones, Chancellor Schmidt, without whom the coalition would never have won the 1980 elections, has suddenly become the target for many attacks.

The new spirit of the times brings his party face to face with disintegration. If it wants to survive as a party of the people, then it must somehow contrive to attract the young with their new feeling about the world: the anti-nuclear lobby, the anti-missile demonstrators, the ecologists, and those who are longing for peace. It is estimated that 25 per cent of young people belong to these movements. But the more you try to integrate the fringe protest groups, the more you risk antagonizing the core of the Party – the conservative workers.

Of course this is primarily a problem for the Party Chairman, Willy Brandt – incidentally the only person who might conceivably solve it. But for Helmut Schmidt the question of whether and how he is to continue governing depends on this solution. It is hard enough to govern when there is no growth and nothing to hand out but only cuts and closures to announce and if, on top of that, there is a general feeling of unhappiness and political discontent, then a statesman of genius is required to master the situation. Helmut Schmidt has given many examples of his talent and energy: now he faces the final test.

And what about the new spirit of the age? Is it really so new? Are the symptoms we see really a characteristic of the spirit of the age? Or are they fleeting phenomena like the movements that arose around Pierre Poujade in France in the middle fifties, or around Mogens Glistrup in Denmark in the middle sixties?

The spirit of our times is represented not so much by a movement as by a multitude of grievances coming together. Uneasiness about the world as it is, dissatisfaction with our society, anti-nuclear feelings, criticism of the capitalist system, hostility to industrial growth, scepticism about technology, cultural pessimism. None of these are spontaneous reactions or transitory feelings: they are the precipitate of intellectual developments over more than a generation. Aldous Huxley's prophetic parody of technocracy, *Brave New World*, appeared in the early thirties, and at the end of the fifties Galbraith wrote his lucid work of economic criticism, *The Affluent Society*. Shortly after, Rachel Carson followed with her epoch-making book *The Silent Spring*. And in the seventies people were shaken up and excited by the Club of Rome and its discussions.

Not surprisingly, the reaction has been particularly strong in the Federal Republic. After the Second World War Germany was in a special situation: her cities destroyed, her people disturbed, twelve million refugees squeezed into what was left of Germany. For years afterwards all thought and energy had to be directed exclusively towards rebuilding, production, action, and cost effectiveness: spiritual, cultural, human and emotional values were neglected – and had to be neglected. The result is that now the young have been seized by ideas that have exercised and agitated intellectuals for half a century, from Huxley to the Club of Rome. Many of these young people are caused real suffering by the crisis in the ecology, and by commercialization and technology invading their lives.

These young people care more about senses and feelings than about sober rationality. This opens up new possibilities, but it also threatens old perils. Pragmatic action will no longer suffice. Spiritual leadership is needed. For in such times pragmatism without wider horizons can easily lead to opportunism and cynicism.

References

1   A. Lowe, 'Die Hoffnung auf kleine Katastrophen', *Die Zerstörung einer Zukunft – Gespräche mit emigrierten Sozialwissenschaftlern*, Hamburg, 1979

2   A. Grosser, *Deutschlandbilanz, Geschichte Deutschlands seit 1945*, Munich, 1970

3   S. Haffner, *The Rise and Fall of Prussia*, London, 1980

4   H. Richter, *Zwischen Freiheit und Quarantäne*, Hamburg, 1961

5   P. Weymar, *Konrad Adenauer*, Munich, 1955

6   G. Mann, *Zwölf Versuche*, Frankfurt, 1973

7   G. Gaus, *Zur Person*, vol. 2, Munich, 1964

8   A. Baring, *Aussenpolitik in Adenauers Kanzlerdemokratie*, Munich, 1969

9   H. Blankenhorn, *Verständnis und Verständigung*, Propyläen, 1980

10 Ibid.

11 Baring, op. cit.

12 Gaus, op. cit.

13 Andreas Hermes, Anna Hermes, *Und Setzt Ihr Nicht Das Leben Ein*, Stuttgart, 1971

14 Blankenhorn, op. cit.

15 K. D. Erdmann, *Adenauer in der Rheinlandpolitik nach dem ersten Weltkrieg*, Stuttgart, 1966

16 K. Adenauer, *Erinnerungen*, 4 vols, Stuttgart, 1965–78

17 Baring, op. cit.

18 Adenauer, op. cit.

19 Ibid.

20 Ibid.

21 Ibid.

22 W. G. Grewe, *Rückblenden – Aufzeichnungen eines Augenzeugen deutscher Aussenpolitik von Adenauer bis Schmidt*, Berlin, 1979

23 C. B. Bohlen, *Witness to History, 1929–1969*, London, 1973
24 Grewe, op. cit.
25 Adenauer, op. cit.
26 Ibid.
27 Ibid.
28 Ibid.
29 Ibid.
30 Grewe, op. cit.
31 *Untersuchungen und Dokumente zur Ostpolitik und Biographie*, Edited by Rudolf Morsey and Konrad Repgen, Mainz, 1974
32 F. Fischer, *Grisf nath der Weltmasct*, Dusseldorf, 1962
33 Baring, op. cit.
34 A. Baring, *Sehr verehrter Herr Bundeskanzler! - Heinrich von Brentano in Briefwechsel mit Konrad Adenauer, 1949–1969*, Hamburg, 1971
35 W. Schlickling, 100 *Jahre Jung*, Wiesbaden, 1964
36 J. Rueff, *Politique économique* (Voll. III of *Oeuvres Complétes*), Paris, 1980
37 M. Caro, *Der Volkskanzler Ludwig Erhard*, Cologne, 1965
38 W. Besson, *Die Aussenpolitik der Bundesrepublik Deutschland - Erfahrungen und Massstäbe*, Munich, 1970
39 M. G. Dönhoff, *Deutsche Aussenpolitik von Adenauer bis Brandt*, Hamburg, 1970
40 W. Brandt, *Begegnungen und Einsichten, die Jahre 1960–1975*, Hamburg, 1976
41 C. Stern, *Willy Brandt*, Hamburg, 1975
42 *Was hält die Welt von Willy Brandt?*, Hamburg, 1972
43 A. Grosser, op. cit.
44 Stern, op. cit.
45 H. Krempt, *Hart am Wind - Helmut Schmidts Politische Laufbahn*, Einführung Marion Gräfin Dönhoff, Munich, 1978
46 Gaus, op. cit.

Index

205

206